Prais
It's All

"A profound and accessible guide to integrating spirituality into everyday life, It's All Magic offers a holistic approach to personal growth that's both enlightening and empowering. Each daily lesson is a portal to a higher state of consciousness. This is a must-read for anyone wanting to level up their self-awareness and spiritual growth."
— **Bunny Michael,** author of Hello, Higher Self

"Aliza is a brilliant, wise, and truly unique astrologer, capable of weaving beauty, art, myth, and practical guidance that strikes you to the bone. It's All Magic is the perfect addition to any budding (or seasoned) witch who might be looking for accessible ways to bring magic into their daily lives."
— **Lindsay Mack,** creator of Tarot for the Wild Soul

"Aliza is the very definition of practical magic. [She's] a bounty of insight and It's All Magic is a gem! An absolutely perfect addition to your daily practice."
— **Jamie Varon,** author of Radically Content and Main Character Energy

"Aliza Kelly's book, It's All Magic, is not just a theoretical exploration of spiritual topics. It's a practical guide that takes you on a 365-day journey of self-discovery through intuition, tarot, astrology, magick, and more. As you progress, you'll develop daily rituals and magical habits that are not only easy to incorporate into your life but also empower you to create a better life. Aliza's down-to-earth delivery helps even total newbies develop the confidence to manifest their dreams."
— **Theresa Reed**, author of *The Cards You're Dealt*

"*Inspiring and actionable,* It's All Magic *is a valuable guide for people looking to add more enchantment to their everyday life.*"
— **Annabel Gat**, author of *The Moon Sign Guide* and *The Astrology of Love & Sex*

"When things are chaotic, Aliza Kelly's approachable, empathetic, insightful, fun (so much fun!) writing about astrology—and the ways it can help us understand and cope with all the mess and the even messier vibes—makes them feel a little less so. And to have her insight in your hands every day all year long? I feel better already."
— **Jen Ortiz**, *The Cut* deputy editor

It's All Magic

Also by Aliza Kelly

This Is Your Destiny

Starring You

The Mixology of Astrology

There Are No Coincidences

It's All Magic

365 Reflections on Astrology, Tarot and Manifestation

ALIZA KELLY

HAY HOUSE
Carlsbad, California • New York City
London • Sydney • New Delhi

Published in the United Kingdom by:
Hay House UK Ltd, 1st Floor, Crawford Corner,
91-93 Baker Street, London W1U 6QQ
Tel: +44 (0)20 3927 7290; www.hayhouse.co.uk

Published in the United States of America by:
Hay House LLC, PO Box 5100, Carlsbad, CA 92018-5100
Tel: (1) 760 431 7695 or (800) 654 5126; www.hayhouse.com

Published in Australia by:
Hay House Australia Publishing Pty Ltd,
18/36 Ralph St, Alexandria NSW 2015
Tel: (61) 2 9669 4299; www.hayhouse.com.au

Published in India by:
Hay House Publishers India, Muskaan Complex,
Plot No.3, B-2, Vasant Kunj, New Delhi 110 070
Tel: (91) 11 4176 1620; www.hayhouse.co.in

Text© Aliza Kelly, 2024

The moral rights of the author have been asserted.

All rights reserved. No part of this book may be reproduced by any mechanical, photographic or electronic process, or in the form of a phonographic recording; nor may it be stored in a retrieval system, transmitted or otherwise be copied for public or private use, other than for 'fair use' as brief quotations embodied in articles and reviews, without prior written permission of the publisher.

The information given in this book should not be treated as a substitute for professional medical advice; always consult a medical practitioner. Any use of information in this book is at the reader's discretion and risk. Neither the author nor the publisher can be held responsible for any loss, claim or damage arising out of the use, or misuse, of the suggestions made, the failure to take medical advice or for any material on third-party websites.

A catalogue record for this book is available from the British Library

Tradepaper ISBN: 978-1-83782-344-4
E-book ISBN: 978-1-83782-346-8
Audiobook ISBN: 978-1-83782-345-1

Cover design: Jordan Wannemacher
Interior design: Julie Davison

This product uses responsibly sourced papers and/or recycled materials. For more information, see www.hayhouse.co.uk.

Printed and bound by CPI Group (UK) Ltd, Croydon CR0 4YY

*For my daughter, Talula,
whom I carried while writing this book.
Thank you for helping me find the words.*

— AK

INTRODUCTION

Over the years, I've received countless messages from people around the world asking how to cultivate a mystical practice.

- ✦ What does it mean to follow my intuition?
- ✦ How can I work with the lunar phases?
- ✦ How do I interpret tarot cards?
- ✦ Are there any easy manifestation rituals I can try?
- ✦ How do I live a more enriching, spiritually guided life?

Believe it or not, spirituality is built on the small choices we make every single day. The amazing thing about magic is that it's everywhere. Magic is our habits, routines, and schedules. Magic is the way we walk, talk, and greet ourselves in the mirror. Magic is the food we eat. Magic is involuntary inhales and exhales. Magic is refracted light that decorates ordinary spaces with twinkling prisms at the most unexpected moments. Magic is ritual. Magic is archetypes. Magic is rhythm. *It's all magic.*

When you tap into a metaphysical vibration, your daily alchemy, you shift from a passive observer to an active participant—learning, growing, and healing. And when you transform your curiosity into a practice, committing to a cadence, incredible things start to happen. You fortify connections with the deepest parts of your truth, and confidence begins to bloom. Inspired imagination emerges as creativity surges. Abundance bursts through the floorboards. And, over time and all at once, your hopes and dreams transform into tangible, lived experiences. You feel accomplished, fulfilled, at ease—it's what your soul has always wanted.

> It's why your soul chose you in the first place.
> It's what your soul knew you were always capable of generating.
> It's what your soul has been waiting for.

Loaded with 365 thought-provoking exercises, prompts, insights, and musings to help you develop a nuanced spiritual practice, *It's All Magic* is your guide back home. Make it your companion for an entire year—the year your life will change—and read it as a daily devotional nested into your morning routine or nighttime ritual. You can also devour it in larger bites; perhaps you want to explore your own pattern, like reading three entries per day, or seven, or until your eyes get tired. If you choose, you can experience it as an oracle: ask a question, open a random page, and unearth the divine wisdom. Within *It's All Magic*, powerful metaphysical concepts and spiritual breakthroughs become the framework for everyday life.

With that initiation, you're now ready to enter the sacred world of limitless possibilities. It's here, in this mystical domain, that you're free to experiment. To investigate. To craft your own narrative. To feel what it's like to be you—courageously and unapologetically. To nourish both the tiny sparks and the ferocious flames. To be fully, completely here right now. Don't forget, only the present moment contains life.

Welcome to your magical practice.

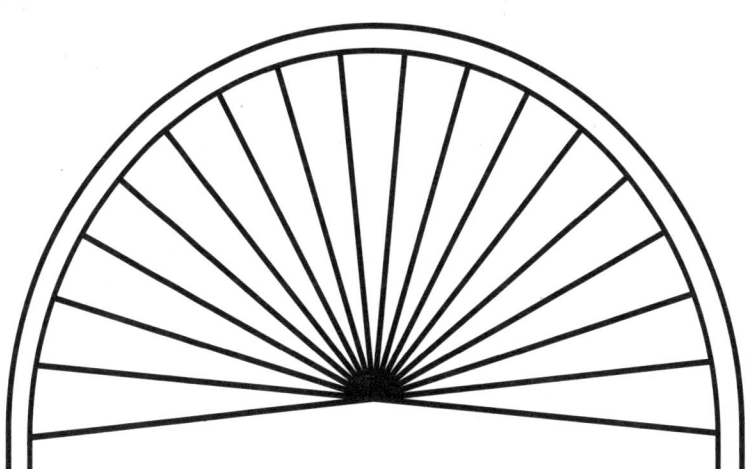

The Messages

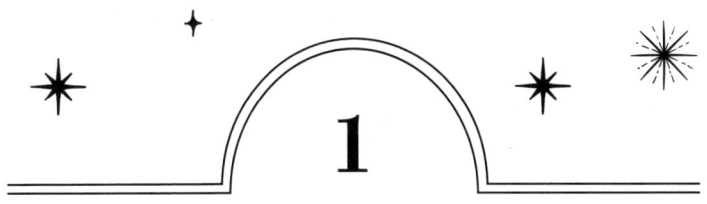

1

Magic is unexpected alchemy. It's the strange, slippery muck at the bottom of the lake: sludgy, slimy, and riddled with hazardous bacteria. It's the fuzzy mold that suffocates ripe fruit. It's the gunk that oozes from wounds. Indecent, unpleasant, and often unruly, magic is the primordial matter that spawns life. Magic is the ancient functions of nature. And magic is in your bones.

2

The Sun represents your ego, your identity, your sense of self. The Sun exposes how you shine, take up space, and need to be seen. It's how you show up, navigate, and move through the world. It's how you face the day. It's where you get your energy. It's how you radiate and find empowerment. It's what makes you feel illuminated, cared for, recognized, and appreciated. The Sun exposes how you arrive, act, and navigate your reality. Today, consider what your Sun sign is and all the ways that you embody it. Contemplate what the Sun means for you on a day-to-day basis. How do you feel when you are greeted by this bright, beautiful star? When do *you* feel like a bright, beautiful star? What makes you feel like your most vibrant, vivacious, dynamic self? Today, explore what it means to embody the Sun.

Authenticity is more important than approval.

4

Everything is constantly in flux. Nothing is the same from day to day, hour to hour, minute to minute, second to second. The cells in our body are constantly moving through their own microevolution, which means we, too, are forever in flow. We are an endless stream. We are erosion. We are creation. No two gusts of wind, no two smells, no two smiles, no two experiences are identical. We are constantly in a state of transformation. So even when life feels routine, tired, and repetitive, find the ways that the mundane, too, has changed. Even recognizing boredom signals a shift within our experience. Today, consider how things are different from how they were yesterday and relish that metamorphosis. You are not stuck.

The Fool is the first card in the Major Arcana of a tarot deck, and it depicts an individual who is about to step off a steep cliff. Now this, of course, could be terrifying. Obviously, there are risks and dangers and threatening consequences on the other side of this drop. But the character in the Fool card is unbothered. In fact, the Fool is in a blissful state of wonder. The Fool card signals a time to take a leap of faith. It invites us to step into the unknown. It gives us permission to try something new, to embody the essence of the Fool, the beginner, the naive one, which enables us to approach a situation from a completely new and innovative perspective. The Fool card wants us to find the courage to go beyond restriction, to enter a state of childlike innocence. Today, consider how you can embody this powerful, seminal archetype.

6

What a gift it is to change your mind. What a blessing to be able to shift your narrative, to transform your perception, to imagine life is one way and then be surprised when it turns out to be marginally, totally, or radically different than you expected. What an incredible treat to be able to see things from a new vantage, no longer clinging to outdated narratives. What a joy to be able to spread out, stretch, widen the expanse of your horizon, and look at something with a fresh set of eyes. To understand the world with new compassion and empathy and connection. What an amazing pleasure to prove yourself wrong. To adapt, evolve, transform. Today, I invite you to change your mind about something. It could be large, it could be small. But give yourself permission to look at a situation differently and see the ripple effect of that shift in perspective. See what it illuminates and opens within you. See what extraordinary potential is available when you give yourself permission to broaden, to deepen, to evolve.

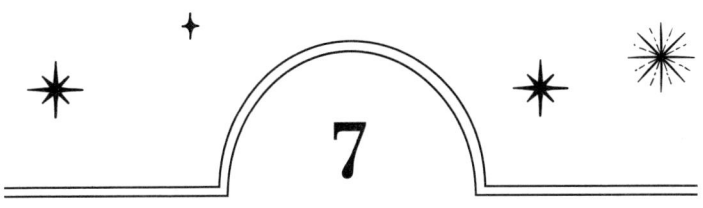

Manifestations work because the process is simple. When we manifest, we place a directive in the physical plane—the realm of tangible, identifiable, concrete objects, experiences, and circumstances—and move that intention into the astral plane. The astral plane is where dreams, hopes, wishes, and ideas exist. It operates in tandem with the physical world. Although what inhabits the astral plane cannot be physically touched, it informs everything that exists in our physical dimension. Everything that exists starts as an idea—and all ideas are formed in the astral. So when we create a directive in the physical realm and send it into the astral realm, we create an infinite feedback loop between these two spaces. We move through the infinite feedback loop to bring wishes into real life. Right now, think about how you relate to the physical and astral realms. What is it like to move between these two intertwined domains? What manifestations are you moving through this feedback loop?

8

If all your wildest dreams
came true tomorrow,
would you be ready
to receive the blessings?

In tarot, the Ace of Wands begins the Wands suit. This card depicts a hand emerging from a sprouts greenery. Delicate leaves fall from the wand, suggesting motion and vibration. There's a phallic nature to this imagery; a symbol of the passion and lust for life embedded within this suit. Wands are about desire, excitement, creativity, and veracity. Accordingly, the Ace of Wands reflects the raw, unabashed connection to creative source, fertile ideas, and sensual desires. This card is seductive as much as it is artistic; it's about having a thirst for life and a deep passion to start new artistic and creative endeavors. Today, consider what the Ace of Wands means for you. What exciting, passionate, romantic, artistic, creative, imaginative stories can you tap into? What can you begin? What can you fortify? What can you enhance? What does this unapologetic desire mean and look like for you?

10

It's normal to seek answers during times of uncertainty. We may look up to the stars, pull tarot cards, or go inward, sourcing insight from our intuition. Sometimes that might do the trick; your inner wisdom foresees exactly what will transpire and proudly illuminates a clear path ahead. But, other times, that deep knowing will feel like unknowing. It will feel like silence, like questions, like nothing. So, what happens when your intuition draws a blank—is it broken? No, it's functioning exactly as it should; sometimes your intuition simply wants you to have faith, to believe, to trust. To learn *from* the challenging and thorny lessons that sprout organically from a life well lived. Remember, your job isn't to get better at predicting the future—it's to become more embodied in the present moment.

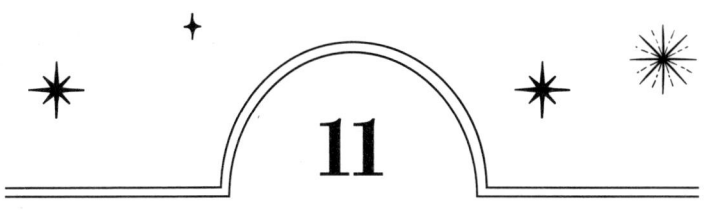

Today, find yourself in a cozy corner—it could be a dimly lit nook with a cup of chamomile tea or your dining room table with a glass of pinot noir. Or, if a quiet space isn't available, the rumbling of a subway on your evening commute or the liminal space between incessant newborn cries will also do the trick. All you need is a journal and pen (or the notes app on your phone, if you're really in a pinch). Set your timer for three minutes and answer the question, "Who am I?" Give yourself permission to explore. If you don't know what to write, write about that. Just keep your pen moving and trust that what you create in this moment is a perfect snapshot of your spirit. It may be profound. It may be mundane. In the mystical realm, there is no hierarchy—both are, will always be, monumental expressions of self. Give yourself permission to be you, right now.

When we speak of alchemy, perhaps no tarot card embodies the spirit more than the Magician. The Magician depicts an individual who has all of the tools laid out on the table in front of them. They're working with resources, with intuition, with strategy, with passion. The Magician has one hand pointed down and the other pointed up, representing the Hermetic axiom "As Above, So Below." The Magician also has a sacred halo in the shape of the infinity symbol over their head, reflecting the divine transmissions they're receiving. Fundamentally, the Magician can do *anything*. The Magician can transform, reimagine, modify, adapt, evolve. The Magician can shapeshift the most ordinary happenings into enchanted experiences. Right now, think of how you can embody the Magician archetype.

Forgive every version of yourself.

14

You don't need to be afraid of your darkness. We all have pain that exists within the folds of our psyche that manifests in insidious ways. We all have habits that resemble vices, behaviors that ignite shame. We've all made decisions we aren't proud of. We all carry heavy weight in our souls. And there's nothing wrong with possessing this dimension, with questioning its purpose. Darkness is an important contour of our existence. It's natural. It's normal. It's an understandable expression of the thorny parts of your journey. Today, find compassion for this, and recognize its place in your life.

A lot of misconceptions exist around the meaning of the ascendant (also known as the rising sign). Technically speaking, the ascendant is the zodiac sign that was rising on the eastern horizon at your exact moment of birth. Some astrologers refer to the ascendant as "the mask you wear in public." But this isn't a comprehensive enough interpretation of the ascendant. The ascendant is your mission. The ascendant is the road map for your entire birth chart and, therefore, your entire life. The ascendant reveals how you see and experience the world. All of the other planets in your birth chart respond to the mission of the ascendant. So, in a way, the ascendant is your vantage. It's not a mask. It's not a facade. It's not a veneer. It truly *is* your experience. Today, think about what the ascendant means for you, both in your birth chart and as a concept. What is your experience? How do you define it? What are the themes that come up time and time again in your life? What is your status quo? What is your mission? How does this mission inform your choices, your relationships, your connections? The way you approach new projects and ideas? The type of experiences you take on? Today, think about what it means to see the world through your eyes.

16

Freedom means different things to different people. For some of us, freedom is hopping on a plane with a one-way ticket, exploring some magical, far-off land. For other people, freedom is the ability to create and manage their own schedule. It's having the time to explore your habits, hobbies, and curiosities. Or maybe freedom is linked to finances—an ability to pay for things without fear or apprehension, the ability to take care of your nuclear and extended family with ease. Or perhaps freedom is self-expression. It's getting to say, do, behave, dress, and act however you would like. Without judgment. Without limitations. Without external or internal criticism. Maybe it's true cultural, religious, or social sovereignty—the ability to exist, as you are and where you are, without persecution. Today, I want you to reflect on what freedom means to you. What ignites a sense of autonomy? What makes you feel like you can truly spread out, take up space, and be unencumbered? Consider the multitudes of freedom, noting which expressions resonate most closely with your soul's unique vibration. Remember, we are not free until we are all free.

Anxiety is a spiral.

Intuition is a whisper.

18

We all have secrets. Things we've done, or things we've thought. Memories, both real and imagined, that live in the folds of our psyche. In my practice, I believe that a deep devotion to the truth—the concept of veracity—is the most sacred expression of spirituality. But secrets and veracity don't necessarily negate each other; ultimately, it's about how you manage your hidden world. Yes, everyone has secrets, but it's important to tend to them in healthy, productive ways. Right now, take a moment to honor your secrets. Give yourself permission to reflect—in a journal or in your mind's eye—on the untold parts of your story that *only* you know. Consider why they exist as secrets and what their clandestine role means in your life. Notice where they live in your body, how often you think about them, and how much real estate they take up in your psyche. Secrets are part of a shared, human experience. There's nothing inherently wrong with them. But careful reflection is an important part of tending to them, ensuring that they're managed, maintained, and not slowly overtaking your subconscious. Secrets require accountability.

The Two of Wands depicts an individual looking out onto the horizon, holding a globe in their hand. Their outfit is traditionally what you would associate with an explorer and, accordingly, this card speaks to discovery. It speaks to expanding our horizons, going beyond our comfort zone, trying something new. There's an exciting wanderlust present in this card, evoking a new idea, a new beginning, or a new possibility. This card invites you to begin a new journey. It reminds you that the world is your oyster—quite literally at your fingertips—and there's nothing that you can't accomplish. Don't limit yourself. Explore further. Think about what you can do to channel the Two of Wands energy today. What adventure are you just beginning? Remember, it doesn't require a passport to be fulfilling. An adventure can look like tapping into a conversation or hobby, or perhaps unearthing a new part of your identity. How can you metabolize that today?

20

How often do you feel like an "outsider"? I do regularly. Chronically. Perpetually. But, ironically, this type of isolation is a very universal experience. I suppose individual consciousness will always create a boundary between self and the collective. Of course, feeling different can sometimes be isolating—even traumatizing. But other times (and, hopefully, often-times) we recognize that our unique sensibilities make us special. That our eccentricities help us stand out and break up the homogeny. That they empower us with a different perspective. A distinctive point of view. A one-of-a-kind way of experiencing the world. Our unique artistic voice. Today, honor what makes you distinctly *you*.

Once you've completed a manifestation ritual, it's important to be aware of what transpires in the days and weeks that follow. Notice subtle shifts. Observe how you feel, what you think, and any patterns or recurring narratives that begin to surface. Pay attention to external feedback, too: Perhaps you received an unexpected e-mail? Or long-standing plans suddenly changed overnight? As your manifestations unfold, you'll start to encounter clues—both small and large—that offer invaluable information. Based on the feedback you receive, you may be inspired to modify or adjust your intentions. Are things moving as you expected? Has your perception shifted? Most importantly, have your desires evolved? Give yourself permission to change your mind and adjust your intentions as needed. After all, you're co-creating with the Universe; flexibility plays a critical role in your magic.

Everything happens at exactly the right time.

The High Priestess depicts an extremely revered spiritual figure situated between esoteric pillars, holding a sacred scroll and sitting on a throne with the moon at her feet. The High Priestess signals a movement toward intuition, mystery, and spiritual philosophy. Conjuring the High Priestess is about trusting your own journey and embodying the divine wisdom that exists within your soul. It's about recognizing the incredible power that you have that no one can take away from you—this innate ability to understand even the most complex, arcane knowledge. Consider how you could channel the High Priestess. What would it look like for you to fully and completely believe in your own spiritual potential?

24

Does starting over feel like the consequence of failure? If so, I encourage you to shift your perspective. We start over every day when we wake up and greet a new sun, a new sky, and a new landscape with new connections, possibilities, and opportunities blossoming in the most unexpected places. Starting over is an extraordinary gift. In what ways can you start over right now? What are the situations, the circumstances, the attitudes, and the actions that would benefit from renewal? Where in your life is there space to begin again? And if you feel that your reality is so fixed, stubborn, and narrow that you can't afford a new beginning, well, my friend, that's all the more reason to greet a new day.

25

Do you want to know something that is always available to you? If you're feeling stuck, if you're in a rut? If you're feeling anxious or nervous? The answer, my darling, is your magical practice. Your daily alchemy doesn't need to be anything elaborate. You can meet yourself exactly where you are. If you only have enough energy to write your fear on a piece of paper and shred it up, that's more than enough; that's a magical practice. If you say out loud some of the things your heart desires, that's a magical practice. If you take a moment to consciously inhale and exhale, that's a magical practice. If you go for a walk and tune in to the sounds around you, that's a magical practice. When you choose to engage with a magical practice, whatever that means or looks like at any given moment, you reclaim agency—and when you reclaim your agency, you can unlock powerful shifts in perspective. Magic is literally everywhere. Today, consider what you can do to engage with it as a powerful, functional tool.

The Three of Wands depicts an individual whose back is toward us. Three staffs are planted in the ground, indicating a commitment to the journey. The Three of Wands symbolizes faith in the path ahead. We have already begun this new storyline, and we're steadily moving toward a totally new reality. This isn't about finding the impulse to begin—this is about sustaining and supporting growth and expansion. Right now, consider what you've already started. What would it look like for you to dive deeper into that pursuit? To connect with it even more, and to find continued purpose as you step forward? What would it look like for you to make dedicated choices that support this direction? How can you embody that energy today?

Old ways won't open new doors.

28

Sometimes it feels like our body gets in the way, as if our physical form is at odds with our soul. Like if we didn't have these oversized meat suits to lug around, riddled with blemishes, wrinkles, aches and pains, sore muscles, and pockets of weight, our spirit would be unencumbered. It would be free to explore, indulge, and experience the life it came to live. But our souls chose our bodies with intention. In fact, you could argue that our physical form was the primary reason that our shapeless spirit wanted to incarnate in this physical form; that our soul sought the life that could only be manifested through the physical experience we know as our body. Your soul adores your body. Your soul needs your body—with all of its lines and contours—to enhance and create its experience. Right now, express gratitude for your body, just as your soul did when it chose to come alive through your physical form.

29

The Moon symbolizes our emotional inner world. It's our truth, our vulnerability, what's happening on the inside. The Moon illuminates our sensitivities, our emotional expression, the way that we feel. The Moon is private. It's sacred. It's intimate. The Moon reveals how we need to be nourished. It shows how we were—or weren't—cared for when we were children. There's a strong link between the Moon and the maternal figures in our life. So today, think about what the Moon symbolizes to you. How do you feel under a new moon, when there is no visibility in the sky? How do you feel under a full moon, when there is electric illumination and the Moon challenges the Sun in radiance, delivering night baths for all who choose to bask in its mysterious glory? What does it feel like for you to experience your emotions, the ebb and flow of those cycles? Today, explore what the Moon means for you.

30

Right now, you're invited to follow your instincts and trust in the Universe's guidance. Life is a mixture of fate and free will; while some events may exist beyond your control, you still have the power to make bold, courageous choices that will—inevitably—shape your trajectory. How can you strike a balance between surrendering to the unknown and exercising agency? Today, you're guided to release any attachments to rigid outcomes and embrace the beauty of life's unpredictability and abundant spontaneity. Trust that even when things feel nebulous and unresolved, you're always moving toward experiences and opportunities that will lead you to growth and fulfillment. Embrace the adventure, roll the dice, and remember that the most exciting journeys always have an element of chance.

Amazing things
happen when
you start believing
in magic.

Today, look for clues. Look for strange pieces of wisdom tucked within the mundane. Open a book to a random page. What sentence stands out to you? Gaze out the window. What's the first thing you notice? Lick your lips. What is it that you taste? Listen to the sounds around you. What do you hear? Let each of these observations become more than just a subtle awareness. Let them transform into mystical insight offering answers, solutions, clarity on whatever it is you seek. Let your day be a divination. Use the information around you to interpret your most existential and practical queries. Let the moment—let this day—become your oracle.

The Empress card depicts an individual seated comfortably, relaxed, lavishly on a throne. There is an ease and an effortlessness to the Empress archetype. The Empress knows her value, knows her worth, and isn't afraid to embrace the comforts and luxuries she worked hard to accrue. Today, consider how you can embody the spirit of the Empress. How you can exude ease and comfort, and a recognition of your ability to unwind, flow, and let things come to you without pushing. The Empress reminds us that we are entitled to a beautiful, abundant life—unconditionally. Right now, explore what that means for you.

What are the qualities that you admire in other people? Is it resilience? Kindness? Humor? Loyalty? Intellect? How do those qualities illuminate pieces of you? Do you admire things that you feel you lack, or do you admire the qualities that you naturally radiate? Are you looking for balance, or are you seeking enhancement? Consider how your opinions and perspectives about others—especially the most important and meaningful individuals in your life—reflect invaluable insight on how you move through the world and connect interpersonally. Today, notice whether these qualities are attributes you would like to cultivate within yourself or if they're sufficiently satiated through your external bonds.

35

When you're in a period of profound growth and metamorphosis, it can be difficult to manage all your hopes and wishes and intentions. How do you open your heart to lasting love, find a professional opportunity that ignites your soul, cultivate lucrative income streams, maintain a healthy daily regimen, and find your dream home all in a single breath? Whether you're overloaded with passion and excitement for the future (a good problem!) or you're ready to radically burst open and start from scratch (also a good problem!), this is an excellent day to start a wishing jar. Think of it like a piggy bank, but for manifestations. Anytime you want to make a wish, write it on a small piece of paper and drop it in your allocated magical container (it can be a vase, mason jar, or even Tupperware). By placing the wish in your jar, you don't need to stress about it anymore—now it's up to the Universe to bring your intention into the physical world.

The multitudes you contain exist for a reason. Every day, consider which version of yourself is best suited for your current circumstances.

The Four of Wands is a true celebration. This card depicts two individuals beneath a wreath, holding bouquets up to the sky in pure, blissful celebration. There's vibrant harmony, happiness, and contentment embedded in the imagery. But what's especially compelling about this card is that—from our perspective—we are on the outside looking in. The figures reveling in their accomplishment are depicted at a distance. The Four of Wands is about holding out hope that, soon, there will be a magnificent acknowledgment and reward for all of the hard work. Soon you'll feel a deep sense of personal gratification and fulfillment for the goal attained, the success well deserved. Right now, think about what your Four of Wands moment would be. What will you soon be celebrating? What is that achievement on the horizon? While it may not be taking place at this exact moment, you are on the path to receive it. Trust the process.

38

Life is so painfully unpredictable. In a way, it's almost overwhelming to realize how fleeting our experiences are, and to know that reality could change at a moment's notice. And that's why it's so incredibly important to navigate each day with kindness, intentionality, and purpose. They say, "Don't put off until tomorrow what you can do today," and while I am never keen on procrastination-shaming—because how else do we all survive?—there's something to be said for seizing the moment, appreciating an opportunity, leaning in to those small, yet remarkably special instances when you can go on a quick walk. Or share something that you're excited to announce. Or call a friend you haven't connected with in months. We must accept the bittersweet truth that nothing is certain. Nothing is guaranteed. And while this ephemerality can feel daunting, today, let it inspire you to find gratitude and motivation for whatever openings are available in your life.

39

Dreams are some of the most magical, mystical expressions of our psyche. While some people are more affected by their dreams than others, everybody dreams—the rapid eye movement (REM) state that defines dreaming is chiseled into our human biology. Typically, when we doze off and let our subconscious take over, we let our mind do whatever it wants. Whether we're leaping off buildings or rocking peacefully on a hammock, we're along for the ride. During a lucid dream, however, you become an active participant in the narrative. When you lucid dream, you become *aware* that you're dreaming, so you can even guide or redirect your narrative while you sleep. Interestingly, preparing for a lucid dream starts when you're awake. Today, set yourself up for a lucid slumber by becoming more tuned in to your physical surroundings. Observe small details, like how your hands or feet feel throughout the day, the way the air ignites your skin, or even how your tongue sits in your mouth. The mental habits you practice during the day continue in dreams, so by becoming highly tuned in to your physical body, you'll similarly become more cognizant of how you exist within your subconscious. Good night!

The Five of Wands depicts five individuals who appear to be in a battle with each other using their wands as weapons. These individuals are wearing fancy clothes and, upon closer reflection, are not actually causing any injury or bodily harm. In fact, they're barely touching each other. There's a performative aspect to the conflict and tension depicted in the Five of Wands. Likewise, the Five of Wands tells us that the "challenges" we're navigating may be figments of our imagination—that there aren't any real obstacles standing in our way. Perhaps we've reached a point in our own story where it feels like we're *expected* to confront a difficulty, but in reality, things are still moving smoothly and according to plan. Right now, consider whether the Five of Wands is showing up in your life. Have you been making things more difficult for yourself than they need to be? Are you creating competition with peers that doesn't *actually* exist? And if so, is fear of failure or fear of success to blame? Consider how you might be getting in your own way.

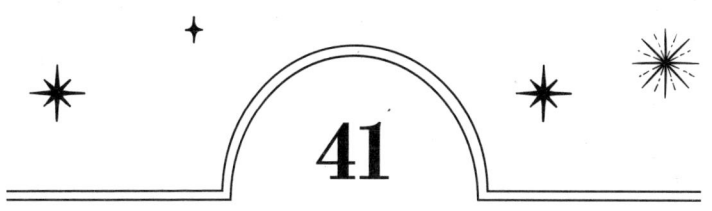

Start with self-love.

Expand from there.

42

When we talk about "inner-child work," we must remember that it's a form of shadow work. Inner-child work is not just about using crayons, playing dress-up, and tapping into our vivid, youthful imaginations. Inner-child work is also acknowledging all of the ways that our younger self felt alone, afraid, or invisible. Our inner children went through lots of raw, powerful, un-intellectualized emotions. As adults, we use our developed cognition, problem-solving tools, perspective, and wisdom to identify situational nuances. Our inner child, however, was vulnerable. We had no defense or armor to protect ourselves from this often harsh and intense world. So when we tap into our inner child, we're not just tapping into effortless play—we're also evoking the wild emotions that emerged from this special developmental time in our lives. Consider what this means for you.

Mercury is the planet of communication. It reflects how we speak, talk, and process ideas. We've all heard of Mercury retrograde, when this swift-moving celestial body appears to go backward in the sky, causing chaos and meltdowns around expression, technology, and transportation (basically all of the things that impact our day-to-day life). But Mercury is more than just a fickle nuisance. In mythology, Mercury (or Hermes) was a powerful figure who would seamlessly traverse domains—bouncing between the world of the gods, the world of mortals, and, of course, the underworld of souls. Mercury was an ally, a chaperone, a messenger who would transport important information back-and-forth across realms. Today, think about the role that Mercury plays in your life. How do you use your words to make magic? What is your connection to language? To dialogue? To self-expression? In magical practices, speaking something out loud is said to amplify its power. Consider what you can speak out loud and how you can sync your intentions, desires, hopes, and dreams with your words, moving these concepts from one realm to another.

44

You're allowed to get things wrong.

You're allowed to be proven wrong.

You're allowed to make mistakes.

You're allowed to be incorrect.

You're allowed to mess up.

You're allowed to be imperfect.

You're allowed to stumble.

You're allowed to move backward.

You're allowed to try again.

You're allowed to apologize.

You're allowed to start over.

Just because it's
not happening quickly
doesn't mean it's
not happening.

46

Who has seen everything and lived through it all? Who has touched every thorn, basked in every delight, believed in every success, and picked you up after every failure? Who has remained in your corner, nourishing your body, watching you grow since birth, since the womb, since the moment your spirit chose your form? Who has tended to your blooming, blossoming, transforming into the person you are today? Who has contributed to your becoming an expansive and radiant being whose profound joys and vast pains constitute a life well lived? It's you. It's always been you, and it will always be you. Know that you are never alone.

The Emperor card in the tarot depicts a ruler who sits confidently on their throne. Direct. Assertive. Autonomous. The Emperor symbolizes an individual who is clear on their identity. The Emperor has a strong sense of self and doesn't bend their will to accommodate others. While flexibility is, of course, important, the Emperor card reminds us that our autonomy, sovereignty, and independence can also be a powerful reflection of our truth. Sometimes simply sitting in our strength is the right course of action. Today, consider how you can embody the Emperor.

48

Although we are constantly trying to accrue experience to legitimize ourselves, our *inexperience* is extraordinarily valuable. Our ability to develop systems, routines, and philosophies that haven't been tainted by overexposure is one of the most magnificent, unique expressions that we can possess. We don't have to feel limited by conventions, mores, and binding structures: we can experiment, invent, and generate brand new ideas that radically shift the status quo. Our greenness on a certain topic or subject is something to revere. It's an opening. It's a pathway. It's a portal. Right now, find gratitude for all the things you don't know, recognizing that these are gateways to extraordinary potential.

While magic serves to amplify and enrich our innate energetic capacities, superstitions hold a suppressive grip on individual potential. Superstitions enforce a uniform doctrine, built upon sweeping assumptions and broad generalizations (take, for example, that black cats symbolize bad luck), fixated primarily upon external variables beyond our control. Superstitions insidiously sever our unique connection to the Universe. Right now, consider what superstitions may be taking over your psyche. Are they innocuous, or are they actively holding you back from living your fullest, most dynamic, most bodacious life? If the latter is true, consider ways you can begin to release those negative feedback loops. Remember, you're not bound to outdated ideology; you can change anything whenever you'd like. That's the magic of being alive.

What you resist,

persists.

51

The Six of Wands depicts an individual who's being recognized and celebrated. Riding a horse, the central figure is wearing a wreath and carrying an elaborate wand decorated in a victory laurel. The energy of this card is about accomplishments and appreciation. It's about receiving the awards, accolades, honors, and access that you've worked hard to earn. Today, consider what your Six of Wands moment would be. What would it mean for you to reach an important milestone? Or for your reputation to reflect your hard work, identity, and truth? What would it mean for you to feel like you're establishing your place in the world? That you're being congratulated for well-deserved success? While we can't always be in a Six of Wands moment, it's important to remember that those experiences are available and accessible to us. More importantly, moving toward that victory, progress, and confidence is a necessary part of the journey.

When you first begin a new creative endeavor, your skill may not match your taste. Think about it: You've had years to cultivate your artistic sensibility. You know what you deem quality work. You know what inspires you. But when you're first beginning the process of stepping into and embracing your artistic skills, you're not necessarily going to have the ability—or years, or resources, or knowledge—of the artists that you admire. But that's a normal part of the process. That should be expected. You should *anticipate* not being as polished as the people you look up to when you're first beginning—you simply couldn't be yet! It doesn't mean that you're never going to be able to match your taste; it simply means that you need more time to refine your abilities. So don't throw in the towel too soon. Know that everything requires patience, resilience, and dedication. Keep going and don't give up.

53

Your magic is amplified through your voice; the melody of your vibrational resonance. These ancient sounds—the frequency of your soul—serve as powerful conductors for your intentions, which is exactly why spells are often spoken or sung out loud. You can also incorporate repetition into your spells through rhymes, which leave deep psychological impressions that help you remember words over long periods of time. You can try it yourself: I recommend penning a simple rhyming invocation that you can repeat several times (for example, "Come to me, so mote it be"). Say it (or sing it) out loud, increasing your volume as you chant the words. Not only does generating a rhythm help focus intention, but the cyclical nature of repetition and vibration builds a dynamic pulse that energetically charges your incantation. You can incorporate this technique into an existing spell or perform this spoken magic as a manifestation of its own.

The Seven of Wands depicts an individual who is working to protect what they believe is rightfully theirs. Stressed and struggling, the central figure in this card is holding a wand as a shield, as they safeguard the six other wands that have been anchored into the ground to maintain their territory. This card speaks to self-defense, protection, courage, and self-reliance. Right now, consider what you feel obligated to protect. Perhaps it's intellectual property, or maybe it's your reputation. Maybe it is an identity that you've cultivated, or a family member who relies on you. Consider whether this type of defensive approach is really required—or, perhaps, if you're conflating protection with obstinance. Are you white-knuckling your current circumstances due to a fear of change? The Seven of Wands may speak to the areas of our life that we genuinely need to preserve, or it could reveal where we are preventing fluidity from taking place. Consider where you stand on that.

Yes, you changed.

That was the point.

We want to be loved or, at least, we want to be liked. It's evolutionary; the survival of our ancient ancestors hinged on the ability to be accepted by a group. To be recognized, valued, protected. And sometimes—even in this strange modern world, which often closely resembles a dystopian sci-fi novel—we revert to these core, primal instincts tucked into the folds of our mammalian limbic system. But you are not just here to survive, you are here to thrive. You have the gift of choice. You know the difference between inspiration and depletion. You know who lights you up, and you know who drains your energy like a real-life vampire. Not everyone is for you, and you are not for everyone. And that is a wonderful thing.

Venus is the planet of love, values, beauty, and worth. When we think about Venus, we can imagine the Marie Antoinette archetype—the energy of desiring luxury, of wanting to be wined and dined, bathed in essential oils, fed delectable sweets, and ultimately worshipped by all adoring fans. Venus is unbothered by the stress and worries of day-to-day life. Venus knows how special and magnificent she is. Venus represents our *wants* as opposed to our *needs*. Venus plays an important role in our life, reminding us that we are allowed to be loved, and that we are deserving of adoration, care, pleasure, and reverence. Venus reminds us that we, too, are sacred. Today, think about what these concepts mean to you. Do you allow yourself to be loved? Do you give yourself permission to be adored? Consider how Venus shows up in your life.

Being afraid doesn't mean that you're not brave; your fear doesn't invalidate your courage. We contain many emotional experiences within our vessels. We're not limited to only the expressions that feel empowered. Sometimes fear *is* empowering. Sometimes it's empowering to know what our limits are and where boundaries exist and where we can push back against ourselves. How can you grow, blossom, evolve, and self-actualize if you can't get in touch with your fear? The things that make us afraid give us insight into who we are, what we need, and where we can continue to stretch, expand, and grow right now. Think about your fears. Hold them. Embrace them. They exist for a reason. Why should you ignore such a special, vulnerable, and intimate part of your soul? In our self-actualization journey, we must remember that there is no hierarchy. All parts of self are important, valid, and meaningful—especially your fears.

Are you moving
in circles, or is your path
an upward spiral?

60

I often say, "You know what you need to know, when you need to know it." In the metaphysical world, we understand information exactly when we're ready to receive it. And this process—of acquiring the wisdom right on time—is nothing short of extraordinary. Just as you're ready to dive deeper into your emotions, you'll be compelled to learn about the Moon. Or, as you prepare to transform your life, you'll pull the Tower card in a tarot deck—the symbol of massive upheaval. The Universe is always punctual, which means you don't need to force anything. You don't need to rush the process. You don't need to try to metabolize insight prematurely. You know what you need to know, when you need to know it. Trust that everything will be revealed precisely when you're ready to receive the wisdom. The Universe's timing is impeccable.

The Hierophant card reflects responsibility, tradition, and stoic awareness. A holy spiritual figure, the Hierophant exudes a serious and unwavering perspective on faith, values, morality and structure. The Hierophant reminds us that even though discipline and responsibility aren't always the most seductive options, there's a time and place for serious, sacred contemplation. Through this archetype, we're reminded that—for others to take us seriously—we must first respect ourselves, treating our values and beliefs with the utmost reverence. Right now, consider what the Hierophant means to you. How can you embody a thoughtful stoicism that illuminates the larger mission you're working toward?

When we talk about building a legacy—fundamentally—we're talking about the culmination of a body of work that defines your professional or creative output over the course of your entire your life. A legacy is the amalgam of lots of expressions of the soul, over many years of hard work and refinement. So not *everything* you produce needs to be perfect. Just as a bad photograph of you shouldn't be measured as the pinnacle of your existence, you don't need to put so much pressure on every single thing that you create. Lower the stakes. Take the stress out of your day-to-day by simply allowing yourself to exist, trusting that—in time—everything will come into place. Give yourself permission to experiment, make mistakes, and learn as you go.

63

When was the last time you safely and consciously journeyed into the profound realm of solitude, a sacred space where inner alchemy unfolds and your spirit finds renewal? Like a hermit retreating to their mountain cave, solitude offers a precious opportunity to dive deep within. Today, create a sanctuary where you can commune with your inner self. Arrive comfortably, and as the external world quiets, let your thoughts drift to the floor. In this hushed cocoon, take a moment to pause and reflect. As you breathe, let go of distractions and embrace the vastness within. Here, you can mend the fractures, refine the details, and receive the insights that arise from the depths of your being. In solitude's warm embrace, you become the alchemist, transmuting challenges into wisdom and isolation into soul-nourishing connection. As you step back into the world, remember the power of embracing your own company.

Trust the process;
all will unfold
as it should.

Interestingly, there is no central figure in the Eight of Wands. This card depicts eight wands moving through the air diagonally, with presumed speed and precision—likewise, this card symbolizes progress, movement, action, and determination. What does momentum mean to you right now? What information would be important for you to receive? What swift knowledge would help you push forward, emboldening you with the confidence to move more efficiently toward your goals? Don't be afraid to pick up the pace if you find yourself in a perpetual limbo. The Eight of Wands is a reminder that, sometimes, it's okay to feel impatient—it's a sign that you're ready for something new. Consider the ways you can take action to expedite your experience.

66

If you feel like you're reverting to an older version of yourself, or like outdated habits are resurfacing, greet yourself with compassionate curiosity. Ask yourself why these behaviors have returned. Did you miss them, or was there nothing to replace them? Did the absence of something new create a pathway to the past? Even if the systems you've outgrown begin to resurface, trust that their arrival may only be temporary. Things may look familiar, but you are not the same.

Today, befriend a neighborhood tree. It could be the oldest one on the block. Or the youngest. Maybe it's a tree with an interesting bark pattern or a different type of leaf. Or one that isn't special or distinctive at all—perhaps it's the most ordinary tree, on the most ordinary block you can find. For any reason (or no reason at all), find a tree to form an alliance with. Greet this tree whenever you walk by. Ask it how it's feeling. How it is experiencing the season. Invite any juicy local gossip or deep spiritual wisdoms it would like to share. And you can offer your secrets, feelings, and experience to it, too. Abstractly, it may seem silly to form a relationship with a tree—but I can assure you, the bond is strong. This unique exercise is a way to harmonize with nature. Inter-species alliance is a microcosm of the macrocosm: your connection to all living beings on this planet. Through metaphysical practices, we discover that we're all bound through breath. Today, find your tree and befriend it.

It's easy to think of the Lovers card in relation to romance, but the Lovers card really speaks to the joy of collaboration. The pleasure of finding someone who gets you. The bliss of being seen, recognized, and appreciated by a safe and familiar friend. The Lovers card invites us to partner, collaborate, share ideas, experience a dynamic give-and-take in ways that inspire creativity, spirituality, and powerful healing. The Lovers card recognizes that finding your match, whether it be through romance, friendship, or professional alliance, is an extraordinarily sacred experience. Right now, think of who your lovers are and express gratitude for their presence in your life.

69

Speak all your worries and fears into a bowl of water. Let your anxieties sink into the tiny pool and notice how the water transforms to absorb your stress. Does it swirl? Does it change color? Does it ripple with every consonant or vowel? When you've poured your last thought into the vessel, dump the water down the drain or return it to the earth. Visualize your stress washing away, moving with the current like a pebble down the river. Let it go.

70

What is your greatest desire? Your loftiest ambition? Your most far-fetched, unrealistic, pipe-dream? What does that goal, that hope, that possibility feel like in your body? How do you physically embody the thing that you want the most? Today, I want you to put aside your judgment, ridicule, shame, self-doubt, criticism—the voice inside of you that says it's impossible. I want you to see what it's like to feel this remarkable desire fully and completely, to let the sensation of that accomplishment light you up. Feed your soul. Excite your spirit. Move the electricity through your veins and—most importantly—let the sides of your lips curl up to form a well-deserved smile. Your biggest ambition exists for a reason. Give yourself permission to foster its magic.

Mars is the planet of action. It's motivation. It's vitality. Mars is anything that we thrust into, which includes sexuality, attraction, libido, desire. Mars is a fierce warrior energy; it shows us how we find determination and strength, and how we behave under pressure. If you're racing to meet a deadline, applying for a competitive position, or moving through a stressful moment, Mars will reveal how you navigate those circumstances. And Mars definitely has a temper—Mars isn't afraid to piss people off. We all know some super Martian people, who unapologetically stir the pot or unleash their anger. Maybe you're one of them! But for others, embracing and connecting with our frustrations, aggression, and fiery spirit doesn't necessarily come easily. We've been told that those qualities are unattractive, inappropriate, or unprofessional. And in certain contexts, of course they are. But connecting with these passionate expressions of our soul is essential and shouldn't be ignored. Today, think about what Mars energy looks like for you. What motivates you? What drives you? What happens when you get angry? How do you process those feelings? Where do they live in your body and how can you move through them? Embrace Mars's fierce and dynamic archetype.

When something pulls your attention, examine it. What's intriguing about it? Is it the shape, the texture, the negative space? Is it the way that it smells? The way that it sounds? Do you like the way it fits in your hand? Pay attention to the specifics and note what captivates your interest. These qualities and characteristics define the style that resonates with your soul. Your awareness of these subtleties will help you clarify your unique preferences. They'll help you identify the ways you aim to enhance and create a beautiful, mystical life. Your ability to investigate the minutiae of your proclivities will empower you to make choices that reflect your own individual artistic and creative sensibilities.

Gut feelings are guardian angels.

74

We cannot force a magical, profound, life-changing experience. We have to wait patiently for its arrival by continuously inviting it into our life. We must hold space for the possibility of a tremendous blessing to arrive and, in doing so, continue to open pathways for its emergence. We keep stepping forward. We maintain a sense of joy. We plant seeds. We work toward goals. And, all the while, we resist the anxious attachment to the outcome. When greatness is ready, it will arrive. And its presence will be clear and distinctive, with no ambiguity. It will undoubtedly change our life. And as we anticipate this tremendous opportunity, we do not want to scare it away by rushing, pushing, and forcing. When that opportunity arrives organically, lovingly, intentionally, it will be worth our patience and all the time we spent dreaming about its potential.

The Chariot card depicts an individual who is brave and courageous, but also protected by their armor. The Chariot is filled with mystical symbols, notably the celestial canopy over the central figure's head and their elaborate belt decorated with alchemical iconography. This card reminds us that we can do incredible things when we feel supported, guided by the elements and our intuition, and have trusted safety nets in place. The Chariot reminds us that we don't always need to forgo our security to forge ahead. Sometimes, being able to navigate with systems in place will enable us to move farther, faster. Right now, consider what those systems are for you. What does it feel like to be stabilized, nurtured, and supported in a way that promotes and fosters growth and guidance?

There's a funny little adage that I've heard a few times, from various people, in different contexts, throughout my life. Here's how it goes: If you're in the market to buy a red car, you'll suddenly start seeing red cars everywhere. In psychological terms, this is referred to as "confirmation bias," which describes our tendency to search for, favor, or recall information that validates our perspective. Even though only 9 percent of cars in the United States are red, we rewire our brains to tell ourselves that truly, *everyone* has a red car. Today, think about how that applies to your life: What are the narratives you tell yourself? What are the stories that continue to surface in your psyche? What are your beliefs? Philosophies? And how can you shift these statements to reflect the life you want to live? For instance, if you keep telling yourself you're unlovable or destined to be destitute, you're going to continue seeing those concepts reflected in your life. On the other hand, by focusing on your radiance, abundance, and good fortune, you'll start to see these bountiful notions mirrored all around you. Remember, confirmation bias means we are always trying to prove ourselves right—even if that conviction is antithetical to our healing journey.

Quick, scan the room for three objects. What do you see? What did your eye gravitate toward? Note the order in which you made your observations. Now, give these objects permission to illuminate the wisdom of your inner oracle. Your psyche selected them for a reason—trust their ability to guide this process. The first object represents where you're coming from. What situation is being addressed? What storyline do you need to unpack? How does this object speak to that experience? The second object reveals what tools and resources you should tap into it. How might the function, form, design, shape, materiality of your selected object bestow this insight? And, finally, the third object reflects the bigger mission. Why is it important for you to access this truth? What is your inner oracle expressing? How does this represent the microcosm of the macrocosm? Don't overthink this exercise—simply experience it. You already know exactly what you need to know.

Worrying won't
make it better,
so why not let go?

In the Nine of Wands, we see an injured individual desperately clinging to his wand, fearfully observing the eight other wands anchored in the ground behind him. Perhaps this individual has bitten off more than they could chew. Perhaps this fight was a lot more strenuous than they had anticipated. Perhaps—after a myriad of disappointments and delays, sickness and injury—they simply need a break. If you've been pushing so hard, but have been hitting resistance and roadblocks, it may be wise to press pause on your efforts. You don't need to drag yourself through the mud unnecessarily. In fact, a strategic break might empower you to look at a situation from a different point of view, to regain strength and momentum that enables you to start over with a sense of excitement and renewal. If things have been taking a long time, and if you're feeling excessively fatigued right now, consider the option of slowing down.

80

How often do you give yourself permission to exist in the unknown? To be uncertain? To straddle two domains—that liminal space between endings and beginnings? It's scary to walk away without clarity about what will come next. To leave a job, a lover, a friend, a city, or a piece of yourself behind. It's scary to create a void. To feel vulnerable. To feel the fear that tugs on your psyche, a fear that ushers you back into those most unprotected, unsafe, uncertain places. But it's in this unknown that extraordinary things happen. While many cannot tolerate the discomfort and return to their alleged safety nets (no matter how toxic or limiting they may be), today you can choose to persevere. To withstand. To embrace the in-between. Trust that, on the other side of this unknown, your strength will be rewarded exponentially.

81

A talisman is an object (often a charm, pendant, or amulet) that is charged with magic and carried (or worn) to amplify intentions. Today, you're invited to create your own talisman. First, choose an object you'd like to infuse with an intention. I recommend a piece of jewelry or small article you can keep in your pocket. What does this item signal to you? Love? Abundance? Acceptance? Confidence? Once you've identified the type of magic you'd like to ignite, close your eyes and hold the object in your hands, imagining its energetic field extending outward and melting into your palms. Repeat your intention out loud—over and over—until you can feel that energy seeping into your talisman. Now you can wear (or pocket) your energetically-charged talisman whenever you'd like to channel that vibration, whether it's for a first date, a job interview, or radiating excellent vibes at a party.

In the Ten of Wands, we see an individual with their head facing downward, carrying an incredible load. This individual has successfully picked up 10 heavy rods but is undoubtedly overwhelmed, symbolizing the tremendous responsibility they carry. As such, the Ten of Wands reflects the duality of success. Yes, you've made it. You've achieved excellence. You've reached the end of this chapter, but now you have new duties and obligations. Now there isn't as much time to relax and enjoy the little things. While it's a wonderful accomplishment to achieve your goal, there's also a genuine heaviness as you bear the weight of your success. Right now, consider what your goals look like and what unexpected responsibilities might arise should you achieve them. What do you need to manage and navigate? Do you have the current bandwidth to do it all? Are you prepared to take on more work, more tasks, more commitments? The Ten of Wands encourages you to recognize the obligation associated with achievement and to incorporate this into your strategic planning. This way, when you do bask in your successful manifestations, you're not caught off guard by the added pressure of these wins.

Your body maps years of existence. Treat every scar, fold, vein, and stretch mark like a badge of honor. You survived. You're still here.

84

Calling all astrologers, tarot readers, spiritual workers. Calling all empaths, healers, feelers. Today, check in with yourself, and make sure your self-worth is not contingent on "fixing" people, or being "of service," or *needed* by others. So many of us come into mystical work because we're naturally skilled helpers—but why are we so good at this? Oftentimes, it's because of painful, deep-seated voids from childhood. It's because, when we didn't feel praise elsewhere, we received it when we were useful—when we parented our parents, solved adult problems, intuited next steps, or conducted our own version of crisis management. And we built entire identities around supporting, healing, and fixing. So no wonder we're good at helping. But that doesn't mean it's necessarily good *for us*. In fact, when we perpetuate the same cycle and seek validation by being needed, strange things start to happen. For some, it can look like burnout, fatigue, and psychic exhaustion. For others, it can look like engorged egos, god complexes, or intentional manipulation. So, right now, just be aware, and remember that you're not responsible for others' healing. You can assist, you can support—but fundamentally, healing is personal. At the end of the day, we can only ever heal ourselves.

Passion sprouts

straight from

the soul.

86

I hope you're excited about the future, about all of the magical blessings that are waiting for you, about all of the opportunities eager to unfold. I hope you're excited about everything you don't know, about the lessons, the growth, the progress, the wisdom. I hope you're excited about all the ways your life can change through miracles, about circumstances weaving together in this alchemical process, gifting you with everything you could have ever hoped for, and more. I hope you're excited about all of the beautiful opportunities that are waiting for you and about all the ways the Universe is conspiring in your favor.

If you've been redirected, trust that it was with intention. You're being guided to a new path for a reason.

Fundamentally, the highest form of spirituality is surrender. Surrender doesn't mean giving up or giving in—surrender is embracing your divine protection. Surrender is trusting that the Universe is conspiring in your favor. Surrender is knowing that control is (and has always been) an illusion. Control is ego, bondage, anxiety. So when we surrender and release control, we anchor ourselves in the present. We connect with a universal order that's richer, wider, and more beautiful than we could ever comprehend. Because we are all part of something extraordinarily magical, profound, sacred. Today, experiment with the sensation of letting go.

Truth is power.

90

Today, instead of writing a to-do list, write an I-did list, taking a moment to acknowledge and honor your accomplishments. Don't worry, you won't lose track of everything still pending—but this practice may help you gain an important perspective and honor your achievements in real-time.

91

Not all of your passions need to be public—they don't need to be on display for everyone to see, applaud, and praise. Your passions aren't a popularity contest. Keep them pure. Keep them protected. Keep them sacred. They are, after all, expressions of your soul.

In the Strength card, a divinely guided central figure (their connection to the divine is indicated by the infinity halo above their head) is interacting with a large, orange lion. One hand is pressing against the lion's snout, and the other is holding its chin, a pose that symbolizes both physical and emotional strength. The lion is in a state of comfort and bliss: tongue sticking out, tail between its legs, bottom pressing upward. The lion is at total and complete ease in the hands of this courageous protector. This card signals fortitude, bravery, courage, tenacity, and the ability to navigate even the most difficult circumstances. This card reminds us that we have the strength—emotional, spiritual, physical—to achieve extraordinary things against all odds. Consider how you embody the Strength card and where this energy is showing up in your life right now.

The Page of Wands depicts an individual who cannot be missed. Wearing an elaborate ensemble (complete with a feather in his cap), the Page of Wands stands in front of three pyramids—a desert backdrop—while contemplating greenery sprouting from his oversized staff. This card is about looking good and feeling good. It's a symbol of passion, dynamism, pleasure, and decadence. When this card appears, we must remember the adage, "Dress for the job you want, not the job you have." Imagine yourself living your ideal life. What does that entail? What does that look like? How do you move through the world when you are in full and complete alignment with your happiness? Explore what it means to channel that energy today. Experiment with style, language, sentence structure. Give yourself permission to have fun as you embody a very fabulous future you.

94

Not all dark, damp, isolated spaces are alike. Both caves and tunnels may have similar shapes and forms, but their respective symbolism is very different. Caves are endless underground chambers with a singular entrance. When we enter a cave, we're prompted to retreat and reflect—to seek guidance and wisdom through stillness. When we emerge from the grotto, we leave from the same passageway we entered—only this time, we've transformed from the inside out. Tunnels, on the other hand, are meant for motion. As we do not exit from the same place we entered, a tunnel is intended to catalyze change through continuous movement; to depart, we must move forward. We must keep going. Right now, consider whether you're currently in a cave or a tunnel, and what alchemy you're extracting from this sacred, spiritual sanctuary.

Not everyone can be excellent at everything. It's impossible. Certain people have certain innate skills, and those abilities won't necessarily come naturally to you. Today, accept that. Today, redirect your attention from your ineptitudes, to the talents and abilities that flow straight from your soul. Make a short list—between three and five things—that come easily to you. These gifts can be creative, interpersonal, or downright niche. Don't overthink it. How can you strengthen these wonderful qualities? Mature them? Invest your precious time and electric energy into the extraordinary abilities that define your spirit? Focus on what you have—don't dwell on what you don't have—and continue to pour into those vibrant resources that reflect your unique soul.

The Knight of Wands depicts an individual riding a horse in full armor—wearing an extravagant yellow robe and a helmet with fiery orange plumes that undulate in the wind—looking forward as they carry their wand. This card is about momentum, energy, and enthusiasm. It reminds us that when we are in pursuit of an idea, we have the motivation and the stamina to do incredible things. Inspiration is a powerful, energetic conduit that comes in all shapes and sizes, but once you feel it, it boasts an infectious, almost addictive quality. Right now, consider what you're inspired by. Is it an artistic vision? A new crush? The possibility of opportunity? Find your inspiration and let it ignite you from the inside out.

You're always home.

Healing is personal, autonomous. It's one of the highest vibrations of individual self-actualization. And this is why it's deeply egotistical to impose healing upon others—to rob someone of their personal journey by taking responsibility for their growth. Instead, we must focus on healing ourselves and, when we do, we become beacons of light for others who are on their individual paths. We can offer guidance, compassion, support. We can offer mystical services, ritual, and release. But to think *we* can heal others is a slippery slope. People heal themselves.

99

Jupiter is the planet associated with luck, expansion, and fortune. I often refer to Jupiter as "casino daddy"—the archetype of a gregarious, gold chain- and Hawaiian shirt-wearing, roulette table aficionado who attracts an incredible crowd with their big spending, raucous laughter, and—of course—rounds of drinks on the house. Jupiter wants more. And wherever Jupiter shows up in our life is where we can tap into the essence of expansion. Of course, more doesn't always translate into the most positive experiences. Since Jupiter amplifies *everything* it touches, it can also tend toward extremism or overindulgence. But Jupiter reminds us that life is fun and joyful, and that not everything needs to be taken so seriously. That maintaining pleasure, curiosity, spontaneity, and optimism should be part of our soul's expression. Today, think about how you embody Jupiter. Where does it show up in your life? If you're struggling to connect with this energy, consider ways you can call in your own Jupiterian soul.

100

Over and over again, I encounter people who tell me that they aren't creative, that they don't identify as artists, that they don't have an imagination. And over and over again, I call bullshit on that assessment. Not only does creativity define the human experience—distinguishing us from other animals—but souls are *inherently* creative. Your spirit, which animates your body, has a natural preference for symbolism, patterns, emotions, vibrations, abstract thought—all varieties and modalities of artistic expression. So today, resist the urge to define creativity within the terms of process; instead, embrace the ways your spirit interacts with the world through your likes and dislikes, your connection to nature, your senses, and all the sensations that electrify your being in ways that can't always be defined. Embrace your intrinsic artistry.

Only the present moment contains life.

Not everything that feels good is good for you. Remember: we have strange psyches that are layered with juxtapositions and contradictions, hypocrisies and crossed wires. We cannot always rely on ourselves, our first instincts, our impulses to know what's going to benefit us long term. Sometimes, what feels right in the moment can generate pain and destruction. It can push us back into habits and patterns that don't support our highest selves. Sometimes, what *doesn't* feel good is what *is* good for us. The courage, determination, and ability to approach something differently—and the strength to create new pathways for healing—generates cataclysmic returns. It might be uncomfortable. But it might be worth it.

The Queen of Wands depicts Her Highness on an ornate throne decorated with lions and foliage. Holding a sunflower in one hand and a sprouting wand in the other, a wirey black cat sits at her feet. This card speaks to dynamism, passion, and status. The Queen of Wands is recognized for her unique style and vibrant energy—she represents how we light up a room and the aura we exude externally. Right now, consider the impressions you make on others. How does your innate personality shine, radiating the divine presence that only you possess? What does it mean to exude your kind of essence? How can your energetic expression be one of the defining parts of your character? Consider how you embody the Queen of Wands' dynamic spirit.

Today, tune in to something you haven't noticed before. Maybe it's the way that the air feels on your skin, a certain look your pet gives you, the sound your feet make as you shuffle across the room. Notice something that hasn't caught your eye before and spend a few minutes exploring what this discovery may mean spiritually, symbolically, structurally. How does this often overlooked information offer a deeper and richer perspective into your lived experience? How might this moment catalyze additional changes that you've been craving? While these observations may seem simple and ordinary, remember that most magic manifests in the most mundane ways.

Today, embark on a journey inward, threading the needle of intuition through the fabric of your existence. Like a tapestry woven with celestial threads, your intuition is a guiding star that whispers secrets of the Universe to your soul. Find a tranquil space and close your eyes, allowing the world's cacophony to fade. Gently explore your mind's labyrinth, seeking the hidden corners where intuition resides. Reflect on moments when a hunch led to truth or a feeling steered you right. Trust in this innate wisdom, for it's the compass guiding you through the maze of life. Journal your insights, weaving together the patterns of intuition that have perforated your journey. As you trace these threads, notice their vibrant hues and subtle textures, unique to your life's design. Honor its presence—the magic of you—let it unfurl, guiding your decisions and illuminating your path with the radiant light of inner knowing.

Every moment, we're moving through dozens of cycles, stories, and narratives. What are some of the recurring themes in your life right now?

The central figure in the Hermit card is an old man with a long beard, robe, and walking staff. Traditionally, this card speaks to isolation, solitude, and reclusiveness. When we first encounter these themes, we may project negative interpretations upon them. After all, doesn't stepping away from society indicate a sort of outcast experience? But the truth is, the Hermit card is about walking away to look inward, grow, and seek enlightenment. The Hermit carries a lantern with a beautiful light source beaming from its confines. When we are consciously introspective, we can experience breakthroughs, genius, and epiphanies in deep, profound ways. Likewise, the Hermit card invites us to find quiet reflection in order to reach new levels of consciousness. Right now, consider how this card may inspire you to find your own moment of escape, retreating to your own sanctuary to create a powerful boundary that has the potential for tremendous breakthrough.

When we set boundaries, we are responsible for implementing those parameters—in other words, we need to shift our own behavior. We need to model the behavior that you want to see reciprocated and actively participate in establishing these new relationship terms. The onus is not only on the other person; you have an important role in this changing dynamic, too.

Sometimes, when we set intentions, we're tempted to manifest big, sweeping transformations. These desires are so large, so incredibly hefty, that they would yield a completely different life altogether. While dreaming big is essential, it's important to remember that extraordinary things take time to come to fruition. Be honest with yourself: What is the likelihood of becoming a millionaire on a random Tuesday (without any idea how that money would be acquired)? Or meeting the partner of your dreams beneath the full moon, when you have no plans to go out and aren't using any dating apps? When we put such impossible expectations on our magic, we're not being honest with ourselves. In fact, we're actually *disrespecting* the incredible potential of the Universe—it's almost as if we're mocking its generosity. So, rather than spend your energy being disappointed in the Universe, direct your focus toward small, accessible changes. Especially if you're just beginning to cultivate a magical routine, your focus should be on building trust with yourself. On getting to the root of your desires. On moving in the direction of your soul. So, set intentions that are within the realm of possibility—that way, you can start to create shifts that scale incrementally. Once change begins to materialize, you'll be able to gradually increase the breadth of your magic.

The King of Wands depicts a profile view of His Majesty wearing a long orange robe and an extravagant yellow and black cape while sitting on a throne depicting lion and salamander motifs. The king looks off into the distance with a stoic gaze. Regal, spirited, and distinctive, this king has an eccentric vibe; he surely distinguishes himself from other royals. While his ensemble may be bold and unusual, his facial expression reveals that it's no laughing matter. This king wants to be taken seriously and, accordingly, wants his vision, his art, his unique style to be revered as well. Today, consider how you can lean in to your gifts fearlessly and unapologetically. You're different from your peers—of course! That's what makes you special! But rather than see your quirks and idiosyncrasies as shortcomings, recognize that they are defining qualities that underscore your talents and gifts. Today, honor your vision and magical oddities.

You're actually healing right now.

112

No one has it all figured out. I know it may seem like there are people moving through life with the perfect morning routine, the perfect skin care regimen, the perfect meal plans, and the perfect productivity—but that perfection is an illusion. We are all fumbling through this strange experience of being alive, trying to make sense of the myriad complexities that come from our wants, needs, and desires. We're all trying to figure out how to not just survive, but thrive, playing pretend in different ways to make sense of life's strange unknowns. You might feel like you're the only one who's struggling, but I can assure you: we're *all* a work in progress. The point isn't figuring everything out. That's an unachievable goal. What you're working toward today, right now, on this journey, is simply a deeper sense of self and the compassion that comes from meeting yourself exactly where you are.

Saturn is the planet of rules, responsibility, and restriction. Saturn has a bit of a reputation in the cosmos. In fact, the Grim Reaper archetype is modeled after Saturn, who is associated with agriculture and thus carries a symbolic scythe. Saturn is maturity, wisdom, and the experience of getting older. Many of us know Saturn through our Saturn return, which is an important astrological milestone that occurs in our late 20s. It's believed that—at this time—we grow up and transform into our true adult self, becoming our own parents. While Saturn can be harsh, strict, and tough, Saturn is also a symbol of commitment. Saturn represents responsibilities. Saturn is our ability to dedicate ourselves to a mission, a purpose, a value. Without Saturn, we wouldn't feel confident enough to sign contracts, to step forward with courage, or even settle into serious partnerships. Today, I encourage you to explore all the ways Saturn benefits you. How do commitment, discipline, focus, and hard work show up in your life? How can you reframe the aging process to unlock its potential through wisdom? Saturn is pervasive—and Saturn is also a privilege. What a gift to get to know how to work with Saturn; it means you're continuing your rotations on this planet, and that is *truly* a blessing.

114

How rare it is to even exist, to stumble through these strange days and mysterious nights. To greet the bouquets of wildflowers, each named to tell stories: forget-me-nots, black-eyed Susans, common selfheal. To see snow fall and taste it on your tongue—almost nothing, but distinctly something. To be a trillion cells, vibrating rhythmically at the frequency selected by your soul, your alchemical radio. To carry wisdom, memories, instinct, and impulse in layers of muscle, tissue, and bone. To know of the ocean. To know of the elephants. To know of the sun and the moon and the ancient gods banished to the stars. To live all this magic is no accident, no coincidence. And yet we obsess over ambiguous text messages, the size of our jeans, our boss's mercurial proclivities, and a future we can't control. Today, return to the wildflowers, the snow, and the impossible odds of your existence—tune in to your radio. That's your song.

Ring, ring! Who's that on the line? It's you . . . from the future! What message does your future-self need to deliver right now? What encouragement, advice, or guidance will you share? Connect with this wisdom, and without overthinking, write down the information you receive. But here's the catch: In the mystical realm, all time is happening in tandem—there is no real separation between the past, present, and future. All the wisdom you'll ever have and need is available to you—all you need to do is tune in and be ready to receive.

Today, you don't need to explain yourself to anyone. No need to prove your reasoning, get them to understand, or try to make sense of timelines, chronologies, actions, or inactions. No need to dip into your archive of experience and unearth all the pain, trauma, and heartache that calcified into today's choices. Give yourself permission to understand yourself on a purely intuitive, spiritual frequency. Sometimes words, analyses, and justifications can water down—or even hinder—the process of creation. Right now, let the energy exist purely in the astral. If you get it on a soul level, that's what matters most.

The Ace of Pentacles depicts a magical, mysterious hand holding a bright, golden coin, signaling a new financial beginning. It reflects manifestation, opportunities, and potential that are unfolding in the physical world. In tarot, the Ace cards are raw, unadulterated energy. When we see this reflected through the Pentacles suit, it reveals a powerful connection to the material world, prosperity, income streams, and possible investment returns. The Ace of Pentacles invites you to trust the Universe and its infinite gifts. Close your eyes and imagine what it feels like to be in true abundance. How can you connect with this concept of receiving, trusting that resources will flow to you effortlessly and freely? Right now, consider the option that this story of divine prosperity is unfolding in real time.

We often hear stories about people "blowing up their lives." And usually, this means making big, radical changes externally that support big, radical changes internally. Sometimes, your entire infrastructure needs to crumble for you to realign with your purpose. But other times, transformation doesn't need to be that volcanic. Sometimes matching your external and internal experiences doesn't happen with a wrecking ball—it happens with a fine-tooth comb. It's careful. It's precise. It's delicate and slow. Sometimes "blowing up your life" isn't explosive. Sometimes it's gentle. Sometimes it's organized. And most importantly, sometimes it takes time.

My first breakup was devastating. I was 16, totally head-over-heels in love, and convinced that my boyfriend and I were going to be together forever. The ending was sudden, decisive, and clinical. This was a formative event in my life; years later, I would recognize it as what established the foundation for my spiritual practice. As I navigated my breakup, I began exploring different daily routines that would help me process the heartbreak. One in particular became a regular evening ritual—I called it a *rejuvenating shower*. Perhaps the most compelling part of the rejuvenating shower is that it was, structurally, no different from any other shower. It didn't involve essential oils, exotic salts, or enhanced products. What made a rejuvenating shower special was simply acknowledging its healing properties. During a rejuvenating shower, my goal was to cleanse myself on a spiritual level, and I would support that in different ways: adjusting the water temperature, experimenting with my breathing, or visualizing my sadness shedding like snakeskin and disappearing down the drain. And it always worked—so much so, I started telling my friends about it. And guess what? We're all still taking rejuvenating showers to this very day. So now I pass the magic along to you. Today, take a rejuvenating shower and do whatever you need to do to step out of the water cleansed, refreshed, and dynamically present. See what happens when you infuse intentionality into your daily ritual—the results are truly divine.

What you see is
only a fraction
of what exists.

121

The Wheel of Fortune card in the Major Arcana reminds us that life is a gamble. So often we try to find answers, solutions, or glean insight ahead of time. We want to know what's going to happen. We want to feel prepared, responsible, like we're in control. But life is filled with risks and rewards—life is never certain. And the situations and circumstances that we find ourselves in are constantly variable. They're moving and changing; they're under indefinite renegotiation. So rather than fixate on the illusion of control, try to focus on surrender. The Wheel of Fortune reminds us that the journey is the destination. That we are equipped to live these exciting, unknown, unpredictable experiences. Right now, think of how you can release obsession with the outcome and simply go with the flow.

We live in a world of not only instant gratification but also high-speed processing. Perhaps we're trying to model ourselves after computers: responding to e-mails before they arrive, generating excessive amounts of content for social media, or "efficiently" moving through emotions before we even understand their origin. We want things now, and in turn we are encouraged to experience the world at hyperspeed. But this alleged "optimization" is not in the best interest of your soul, your creativity, your spirituality, your magic, or your unique alchemy. Today, give yourself permission to slow down. To read sentences twice or even three or four times over. To encounter sensitivities without abrupt rationalization. To let yourself move through liminal spaces that don't offer immediate answers. The point of this exercise is not to stifle your growth, but to expand, widen, and deepen the horizon of your experience. Not everything needs to be a sprint. Life is most beautiful when we take our time.

Today, you're invited to perform a ritual to release stagnant energy, psychic blocks, or anything that's holding you back from progressing forward. Grab a piece of paper and a pen. Settle in an area of your home where you won't be disturbed. Take a few deep breaths and note the weight of your body anchoring you to the earth. When you're ready, write down anything that's unjustly siphoning your magic. Don't overthink—just write. Give yourself permission to be surprised by what comes to the surface. Then, shred the paper into tiny fragments, envisioning that negativity dissolving with every tear. Connect with this physical act, feeling the energy leave your psyche through your fingers as you rip the words apart. Once you're done, discard the paper scraps in recycling, compost, or safe burning.

The Two of Pentacles depicts an individual who's dancing while juggling two coins in their hands. These coins are linked by an infinity symbol, symbolizing infinite possibilities. Yes or no? Stay or go? Take the risk or play it safe? The Two of Pentacles is about weighing the pros and cons of your decisions. It is about managing expectations and recognizing that every reward comes with a risk—and yet, a dynamic balance is needed to ensure forward motion. Right now, consider what you're balancing, what you're prioritizing, and how you're adapting to the multiple opportunities you're navigating. How can you move through the infinite flow of options, and what does it mean to hold multiple truths simultaneously? When the Two of Pentacles shows up as an archetype, we must remember that flexibility is key.

Not every thought or feeling needs to calcify. Let them roll across your psyche like pebbles lapping the shoreline—inhaled and exhaled by the tide.

I've never met a person who doesn't procrastinate. Yes, of course there are people who procrastinate *more* than others—there's certainly a wide and broad spectrum. But we *all* put things off. We *all* delay. We *all* choose to prioritize certain tasks over others. This isn't a moral issue. People who procrastinate more frequently aren't "worse" than people who procrastinate less frequently. When we layer procrastination with shame, it doesn't improve our productivity. It doesn't make our projects, to-do lists, or obligations get done any faster. It just makes us feel badly about ourselves. Today, I want you to shift your perspective on procrastination. Rather than judge, criticize, and penalize yourself for doing what every human does, simply ask yourself why you are facing resistance. Why are you creating a delay? Or dragging your feet? Or choosing other things over the timely tasks? Is it because they're hard, boring, or unsatisfying? Is it because you experience joy in other ways? Is it because they remind you of things you've disliked in the past? Today, meet your procrastination with curiosity. Replace shame and judgment with wonder and see what happens when you approach your truth with kindness.

Uranus was the first planet discovered through a telescope—an incredible innovation. And that is quite fitting for a planet that symbolizes rebellion, revolution, and radical breakthroughs. Uranus doesn't play by the rules—Uranus creates new ones. Uranus isn't afraid to shake things up, to disrupt the status quo, to approach things differently. Today, consider how Uranus appears in your life. Where are you willing to think outside the box to break the mold? To challenge the system? In what ways do you stray from normalcy? From mundanity? From homogeneity? If we all have a shared experience of feeling different, then maybe the subtle eccentricities that define our souls are expressions of our defiance. Perhaps we are best suited for disruption, to challenge things, and to approach the world differently. Today, consider how you embody the Uranian mentality.

How do you tend to your vices? And what do your shadowy impulses do after you've stopped nurturing them? If you find yourself staring into the past, recalling old coping mechanisms or habits you've outgrown, don't be afraid to explore those sharp edges of your psyche. The truth is that those unruly behaviors—imprints of how you once operated—are best suited for memory. These days, your vices can activate nostalgia rather than behavior: a certain song, a distant aroma, or even an unexpected breeze can transport you to another time. And, for a moment, you can feel that spark of evocative excitement. That thrill. That rush. That reckless spirit.

Prove them wrong.

When we're children, the concept of being kind is enforced quite regularly. Be gentle. Share. Include others. We're taught these lessons young, and as we get older, we're expected to continue to implement them. But we rarely meditate on the extraordinary significance of compassion. Or how meaningful it is to go out of your way to help someone navigate a challenging time. Or the profundity of true selflessness. These acts of kindness aren't just significant on a moral level—they directly improve your life. Compassion is an extension of spirituality; it's a direct line to your soul. Kindness will change your perspective. It will shift your values and enable you to step outside your situation and see the bigger picture. Kindness will inspire and motivate you, generating extraordinary abundance across all dimensions. So today, offer gentle compassion to someone you know, or perhaps someone you have never even met. Your ability to do something kind is a privilege.

The Three of Pentacles depicts an individual standing on a workbench showcasing their craft, while an elegantly dressed couple consults the artisan. This card is about teamwork and collaboration, but most importantly, it's about recognition. In the Three of Pentacles, the couple selected this craftsperson—this mason—for a commission. They entrusted this individual to create something meaningful and profound. In the scene, the couple is reviewing the progress of the art piece; the artist is being recognized, honored, and compensated for their work. Today, consider whether you feel recognized, respected, and valued for your talents. If not, why? Consider ways you can feel more confident showcasing these abilities, acknowledging that it's important to be appreciated. Consider who in your life acknowledges your gifts, and find gratitude for the large and small ways they support your work.

You know what you want in a romantic relationship. You know how you deserve to be treated in friendships. You know the salary you should be earning. But these shifts cannot be achieved by throwing a temper tantrum—they need to be mindfully considered, carefully strategized, and thoughtfully executed. Right now, focus on ways you can turn your insight into action, exploring new ways you can cultivate functional systems. You don't need any additional illumination. You know what you desire. Now it's time to come up with a plan.

133

In the hustle and bustle of existence, today invites you to carve out a sacred pause—a moment suspended in time, a respite for your spirit. Amid the symphony of life's demands, grant yourself permission to take a time-out. Find a serene space where you can simply be. Close your eyes and breathe deeply, inviting tranquility to wash over you. Feel the ebb and flow of your breath, a dance that mirrors the rhythm of the cosmos. As you inhale, draw in revitalizing energy; as you exhale, release burdens that stifle your flow. In this suspended moment, let go of the need to achieve, to rush, or to worry. Instead, bask in the sweetness of the present. Engage your senses—listen to the gentle whispers of nature, feel the caress of a breeze, see the beauty in the simplest detail. As you emerge from this sacred pause, allow its serenity to infuse your actions and intentions. Carry it as a reminder that amid life's currents, you hold the power to nurture your soul's growth with each intentional breath.

The words you speak
will build your home.

The Four of Pentacles features a central character clinging to four large coins. One is wedged into the headpiece, another is tightly tucked between the arms, and two more rest on the ground beneath the feet. This individual is certainly not sharing. In fact, this person is absolutely and completely unwilling to let go of what they have. Likewise, this card represents a need for control, a fear of losing material possessions, and a potentially distorted perspective of our values. This card suggests that we may be holding on too tightly, and in doing so, are preventing new opportunities and resources from reaching us. In fact, it's possible that we may be inadvertently making things harder on ourselves by restricting the ebb and flow of abundance. Today, remember that money is a frequency, and if we want to receive prosperity, we need to be willing to connect with its motion, rhythm, and circulation. Don't conflate frugality with greed.

136

Sometimes you'll compare yourself to others, and that familiar taste of jealousy will bubble up in your throat. You'll encounter someone who's doing what you wish you were doing—and you might bemoan this, or be upset, or experience various shades of disappointment. It's normal and natural. When it happens, just be kind: to yourself, to the situation, to the feelings, to the sour taste in your mouth. Because the more you judge, criticize, or ridicule those feelings, the more you'll spiral. The more you'll shame. The more consumed you'll become by the unpleasant sensation. Just let the jealousy wash over you and trust that, sometimes, this happens. It will pass, and you won't feel this way forever. You are okay.

137

Today beckons you to embark on a journey of profound transformation by delving into the depths of your shadows. Just as a candle's glow is most luminous in a dark room, your healing light shines brightest when you bravely confront the aspects of yourself that you've hidden away. Create a sacred sanctuary where you can explore the caverns of your psyche without judgment. Light a candle and let its gentle flame be a guiding beacon through the cascade of your complex, multidimensional emotions. With compassionate intention, begin to explore memories, experiences, or traits you've suppressed or deemed unworthy. Allow the shadows to unravel—like ink swirling in water—revealing the intricate patterns that have shaped your inner landscape. Witness these facets of your being with an open heart, offering yourself forgiveness and acceptance. As you embrace these shadows, you empower yourself to heal and transmute. With each step into the shadows, you integrate fragmented parts of yourself, catalyzing profound transformation. As the candle's flame flickers, know that you've kindled a sacred light within, illuminating the path toward wholeness and self-empowerment.

The Five of Pentacles depicts two individuals downtrodden, injured, crying in agony as they trudge through a dense snowstorm. Down on their luck, there is a sense of deep desperation and hardship as they move through this unforgiving wintry scene. The building behind them displays a stained-glass window, decorated with five gold coins and elegant floral motifs, but the two individuals appear unaware of glowing warmth radiating behind them. Likewise, this card often suggests how we can become consumed by our own stress, pain, and perceived scarcity. The Five of Pentacles suggests that if we are so fixated on what we lack—on not having enough—we won't be able to see the magic unfolding just overhead. Right now, think about the ways that you may feel stuck, limited, or even desperate, and consider how a shift in your perspective may reveal more opportunities than you could have imagined possible.

In Greek mythology, chaos preceded the cosmos. Described as an empty, formless abyss, chaos was the absence of order—a primordial void. Today, remember that your chaos isn't meant to be a lasting state, but rather a launching pad for creation.

140

When we're anxious, it's easy to become erratic with our thinking. We layer negative thoughts on top of each other, creating thick slices of impenetrable worst-case scenarios. We believe that these one-in-a-million odds, these horrendous freak accidents, these unbelievable disappointments could—in fact—be our reality. These are the classic traits of an anxious mind. One thing I do when I find myself in a mental spiral, is punctuate every negative thought my mind creates with something positive, miraculous, or delightful. And in doing this, I create a dynamic opposition. I retrain myself to consider that it is just as likely that the most amazing, extraordinary best-case scenario can be just as true as the nightmarish worst-case scenario. By creating this diametric opposition, I give myself space to meet the truth somewhere in the middle, to ease the paranoia, to quiet the nervous energy, and to remember that—ultimately—projecting and predicting isn't going to change the outcome. Neutrality is the antidote to fear.

141

Neptune—named after the sea god, also known as Poseidon, who reigned over an impossibly ethereal domain—is the planet of illusion and delusion. The ocean, which has historically always represented the psyche and the subconscious, is wildly vast, complex, and quite literally impossible to explore. There's just too much pressure. And this is, of course, the perfect metaphor for our own psyches, our internal worlds, our astral planes. Our ability to connect with the depths of our spirit demands that we access totally different areas of existences. We need to approach exploration with gentle curiosity. Not rushing. Not forcing. Not going too deep, too fast. Art, creativity, spirituality all provide safe ways for us to be able to dip our toes into these other realms. Right now, consider how Neptune shows up in your own life and how you use imagination—along with spirituality—to tap into the deepest regions of your soul. What can you learn about those spaces through your unique, imaginative process? What do they tell you about the thick layers of cosmic, mystical connection that are intrinsic to your being? Neptune can be disorienting, so make sure you're always anchored in reality.

Today, you're called to explore the cascading wisdom that lives within you. To explore the ways in which you're still animal. (Have you forgotten, my love, that you are 100 percent pure, unadulterated animal?) Your senses were designed to help you navigate this world and, in turn, you experience the world through your senses. But it doesn't end at touch, taste, sound, smell, and sight. Intuition also surges through your animal veins—an evolutionary instinct designed to help you connect the emotional dots. Today, you're called to trust your gut feelings and tap into your profound alignment with the primal energies of the natural world. Tune in to the whispers of the creatures and enchanted entities that share our planet. Know that you don't just possess an innate connection to the natural world and its rhythms—you are that vibration. You're nature, baby. Remember how it feels to be wild.

Moving on doesn't mean forgetting; rather, it represents an earnest willingness to foster new energy.

144

Fear of success can be more paralyzing than fear of failure. What happens when everything goes according to plan? When you receive all that love, abundance, and prosperity you've been manifesting? What happens when you need to embody these blessings—experiencing them not just as concepts but as realities? Today, remember that you *can* receive the bounty. In fact, you *deserve* it. When it arrives, you will welcome it into your life with ease. You've prepared for a long time; trust that you will be ready.

In the tarot, the Justice card speaks to what's fair, balanced, and equitable. Justice is depicted not as a concept, but as a person. The central figure in the Justice card is an individual who is sitting on a throne, holding a scale in one hand and a sword reflecting their intellectual superiority in the other hand. Consider that when it comes to questions of what is fair, balanced, and equitable, the answers are determined by the individual holding the scales. In other words, justice is subjective. Justice is a matter of perspective. So while it's important to consider all sides of a story and weigh the different pros and cons, the Justice card reminds us that the circumstances of each situation may tip the scales from one day to the next. So right now, think about who's holding the scales. Do you align with their values? Point of view is everything.

146

I don't know how else to say this... but you're going to die. I'm going to die. We're all going to die. It's simply inevitable. It's part of the agreement we automatically adhere to simply by arriving on this planet. And, alas, these terms and conditions aren't up for negotiation. Personally, I don't think about my impending mortality often—I don't find death's looming whisper to be particularly inspiring. I do, however, find this reality check to be useful: If we know that life is fleeting, then perhaps we should be very thoughtful about how we spend our time. What truly matters? What's truly important? When looking back on your life, what are the experiences, people, and moments that will have defined your beautiful, ephemeral, poetic existence? Today, I encourage you to venerate and honor the precious magic of your life. Focus on what matters and let go of the bullshit. It's simply a waste of your most valuable time.

147

At this moment of my writing, I hear the rain gently tapping on my oven's stainless-steel range hood. A softer, padded sound on the shingled roof, and a steadier whooshing in the background—perhaps droplets on the road—let me know it's really coming down. In the distance, my dog's collar gently jangles, likely from scratching her ear or repositioning for maximum comfort. An appliance clicks on and off in the kitchen (what is that?) and I sip my coffee loudly in defiant disruption. All this in under 30 seconds. Now it's your turn. What do you hear? What are the layers of sound? What energy do the noises communicate? What mood do they set, how might that illuminate your current emotional climate? This is a brief meditation. You are now in the moment.

Let it come.

Let it go.

149

In the Six of Pentacles, we see an elegantly dressed individual holding a scale and dropping crumbs into the palms of two beggars pleading on hands and knees. The central figure appears cocky and confident, and the presence of the scales of balance symbolizes a sense of moral accomplishment. Certainly, this individual believes that they're acting kindly and philanthropically—but when have literal crumbs *ever* been practically helpful? Sure, the bare minimum may help you survive, but it certainly is not a way to thrive. Today, consider whether you're the individual sprinkling crumbs, or you're the desperate, downtrodden figure accepting the bare minimum. You don't need to settle for such meager offerings! You don't need to feel obligated to accept an offer you know is well below your worth! Alternatively, if you're the one doing *the least*, consider amplifying your efforts. Remember that abundance flows to people who are not afraid to tap into generosity.

150

We get activated when someone says or does something we deem disruptive, disrespectful, or inconsiderate. And when we get activated—depending on how we metabolize that energy in the body—we may want to confront that person: call them out, call them in, or address it through conflict. And, sometimes, this can be a really impactful way of resolving an issue or repairing underlying discomfort. But, before you enter this space of raw tension and unfiltered emotion, be sure to ground yourself. Normalize your heart rate, regulate your breathing, and take a moment to experience your feelings independently. Anchor yourself to truth and find strength distinguishing your reaction from your action. From there, you can engage in a conversation that's healing, restorative, and reparative without blaming, attacking, or shaming. Conflict is an important component of interpersonal harmony— but, in order for it to be meaningful, it must be approached responsibly.

Scrying is a traditional divination technique in which you stare into the surface of an object (usually something reflective or shiny, such as a crystal, candle flame, or mirror) to gain insights or receive sacred messages. Scrying is a simple, effective tool you can add to basically any magical ritual. Whenever you want to surpass the mundane mind (the realm of to-do lists, responsibilities, worries, etc.) and gain insight into your deeper energetic state, explore what it means to enter a trance state with this method. You may surprise yourself!

The Seven of Pentacles depicts an individual who is carefully observing his harvest. Seven coins symbolize budding produce, and our central character leans on a gardening tool, observing the bounty. Their face suggests both impatience and acceptance, recognizing that although the harvest is on the right track, it has yet to deliver in full. Accordingly, the Seven of Pentacles is connected to dedication, perseverance, intentionality, and deliberation. It's a reminder that the day you plant the seed is not the day you eat the fruit, and that good things take time. Right now, consider how this relates to your own life. What are you waiting for? What is unfolding for you? What are you hoping to see mature? How are you balancing both patience and acceptance as you navigate this gestation period? Recognize that life is not a sprint, but a marathon.

Surviving means honoring
the full spectrum of feelings—
devouring the good
and embracing the bad.

154

You cannot hate yourself into a beautiful life. Oftentimes we shame or criticize ourselves for not doing enough, for moving too slowly, or for the choices we make that we deem irresponsible. But before you become another punitive, militant voice that bosses around your psyche, consider the fact that positive affirmation is known to be a more effective long-term approach than aggressive punishment. Today, consider what you want the future to look like. What will you be doing? Where will you live? Who will be in your life? What kinds of resources will you have at your disposal? How will you establish this reality when you work backward from an exciting, passionate, meaningful goal? By working with yourself (instead of *against* yourself), you'll find value and purpose in your choices. You'll make decisions that will actively enhance your life and move toward a more exciting and passionate tomorrow. Trust that your motivation will be sparked when you treat yourself with respect.

155

Sure, Pluto is no longer considered a planet in *astronomy,* but in *astrology,* Pluto has a lasting and important role. When Pluto was originally discovered in 1930, it signified an incredible shift in what we perceived to be possible. Pluto's existence was disruptive. It was transformative. It revealed the depth of a universe larger, wider, and more complex than we could have ever imagined. Likewise, Pluto symbolizes transformation, regeneration, and renewal—it's a phoenix rising from the ashes. Pluto is power, control, obsession. Pluto is the intensity of the unknown. Symbolically, it's also linked to the underworld, a domain that sits adjacent to our life here on Earth. Today, consider how Pluto shows up in your reality. What does metamorphosis look like to you? When have you experienced massive upheavals and what have they produced? When you give yourself permission to explore regions that go beyond your everyday perceptions, you can create new universes, new narratives, new storylines that alter your timeline tremendously. Pluto is a force to be reckoned with—but so are you.

When you bask in the extraordinary natural landscapes that define this rich and fertile planet, you may describe these majestic spaces as *perfect*. And they are. Absolutely, totally, and completely perfect. But they're not perfect like a retouched selfie. Or like knowing exactly what to say at a dinner party. Or eating fancy food on a pristine, camera-ready kitchen counter. These social constructs of "perfection" are unknown to nature—perhaps they're not even perfection at all. You see, nature's perfection is in the raw, malleable, fluidity. It's the changing seasons. It's the strange insects sunbathing on ancient rocks. It's the gusts of wind that scatter pinecones across endless fields. It's the vivid colors and intricate patterns. It's the cracks, the fissures, the edges. So, next time you find yourself bemoaning perfection, remember that nature always prefers your truest expression: organic and unfiltered.

Protect

your energy.

158

There are so many reasons why we don't ask for help. Maybe we were ridiculed when we were younger. Maybe we asked for help and didn't receive it. Maybe we adopted the idea that we can do everything ourselves, that we don't need anyone, and that if something is going to get done, it's better that we do it ourselves. It's easy for these traits and qualities to persist and even intensify as we get older. Those initial injuries that came by way of asking for help cauterize into thick calluses that prevent us from being vulnerable. But asking for help is not a sign of weakness. In fact, it's a sign of confidence, self-respect, and self-awareness. It means you know your limits, strengths, and priorities. Today, I invite you to consider where you may need extra support and to not be afraid to ask for it.

In the Eight of Pentacles, we see a craftsperson hammering away at a repetitive task. This individual is building coins, and several are complete, while a few are still in the works. Determined and methodical, the central figure maintains a steady focus as they move toward completion. The Eight of Pentacles represents consistent efforts, dedication, and the value of cultivating a practice. Right now, consider your own repetitive motions. Whether you have a robust morning routine, steady lunar rituals, or a movement schedule, your habits and consistent efforts reflect your lived experiences. When you make a commitment and chisel away at something, you'll eventually see a return. So where are you directing your energy, focus, and time? Is it going toward the things that align with your broader goals, or are you spinning your wheels and placing your resources in wasted spaces? Make sure you are committing to something that feels genuinely inspiring.

What if you intrinsically knew when it was *time*? What if you didn't need to watch the clock and worry about the days, hours, milestones, and pressures assigned by society? What if you knew when it was time to create the way a bird knows when it's time to prepare a nest, the way squirrels stash away acorns, the way a bear prepares for hibernation? What if you're working on a grander scheme, on a greater timeline, and everything *is* going according to plan? Imagine: your narrative is following a cosmic rhythm that's part of nature, part of life, part of death. Rather than taking action to appease the ego through external validation, shape your day to satisfy a richer, wilder system that connects all existence.

Glamour magic utilizes fashion and beauty as tools of empowerment, manifestation, and ritual. Within the realm of glamour magic, anything you use to adorn your body can be wielded into a mystical tool, from your clothes and makeup to your perfume and the energetic aura you shroud yourself in. As you get ready in the morning, choose an intention you'd like to focus on, such as confidence, honesty, or motivation. Next, select clothing, accessories, and/or makeup that personifies that energy. For example, if your intention is confidence, maybe wear a bright red blazer. If you're channeling abundance, perhaps a hint of green eye shadow to evoke that vibration. There's no wrong way to do this; listen to your intuition and experiment with this dynamic expression of manifestation.

When you find yourself clinging to control, be gentle with yourself. At some point, you felt helpless or hopeless, and small semblances of order were all you had. Remind yourself that you're safe. That you're protected. And everything will flow exactly as it should.

In the Nine of Pentacles, the central figure has achieved true abundance, wearing an ornate dress and contemplating an exotic bird perched on a gloved hand. This individual strolls through a lush garden, overflowing with vegetation, grapes, and, of course, nine shiny golden coins. This individual exudes an ease, tranquility, and effortlessness that is truly aspirational. As the only person in the image, the Nine of Pentacles also speaks to financial independence on your own terms. This character has achieved extraordinary abundance by doing things their way. Right now, give yourself permission to visualize what this feels like. How will you know when you have achieved the success that you desire? When you have enough resources? When you are safe and comfortable within the world that you have created? What will it look like for you to relax and accept this bounty? Life is often a strenuous pursuit of more, but the Nine of Pentacles reminds us that when we have reached our goals, we should take a step back and appreciate the beauty around us, every step of the way.

164

It's scary to put something out in the world—the very real risk of criticism can be paralyzing. No matter how hard you work, or how proud you are of your finished product, not everyone is going to love—or even like—everything you make. But bad reviews will not destroy you. Bad reviews don't reflect your value, your efforts, or your impact. They don't represent the difference you're making in the world, the way you're inspiring others, or how your particular perspective struck a very specific chord with someone you'll never even meet in person. Bad reviews are inevitable. The alternative? Never publish. Never share. Never shine. To stifle yourself due to fear is a much worse sentence than a bad review.

If you wrote your own fairy tale, what would it entail? What would the narrative be, and who are the characters? Would it take place in an enchanted forest? A mysterious library? A magic castle? Or would it unfold right in your own backyard—a bewitched perspective on your day-to-day life? What transformation would you experience? What would catalyze this metamorphosis? And—perhaps most importantly—how would your story conclude? What would be the moral? The lesson? The takeaway? What happy ending would you create? Today, give yourself permission to let your imagination wander, enabling you to access childlike fantasies that ignite your inner truth. See what comes up and let that clarify innate desires. Let this fairy tale become your manifestation. The End.

The Ten of Pentacles is the last Minor Arcana card in the Pentacles suit. It's an intricate and detailed scene with many people, animals, and babies camouflaged by ornate robes, architecture, and foliage. An elderly, white-haired man with a long beard pets his loyal dogs and looks on at a young couple with a toddler, who seem to have inherited this generational fortune. Likewise, this card reflects a deep sense of wealth, prosperity, and financial security. Ten gold coins are sprinkled across this image, underscoring the presence of material success. This card is a true depiction of financial opportunity and opens conversations around the concept of legacy. Generational wealth is not just about money in the bank; it's also about wisdom, time management, emotional processing, and all the resources we pass down generation to generation. Right now, consider what you've inherited—whether it be money, talents, emotions, or perhaps trauma—and how it impacts your reality. Is it something you want to build and scale, or is this something worth letting go of?

How do you find your way back to yourself after something throws you off course?

When we're kids and we're asked what we want to be when we grow up, we offer exciting answers. Our imaginations are vast, wild, and impressionable. We're inspired by people, costumes, and innocent concepts about the world. Our conceptions about the way things work that are rooted in youthful purity. As we get older, we become increasingly confined to material data. We learn about salaries. And status. And reputation. We align ourselves with the standards and expectations that seem to fit our imposed external identity. But you can still be whatever you want. You can still explore. You can break molds. You can challenge the status quo. You can reinvent an entire industry. You can—and should—be anything that lights you up. So don't deny the spark within just because this cruel world drilled it out of you. Today, ask yourself that famous question: *What do I want to be when I grow up?*

169

The Fire element is fierce, fast, and passionate. It symbolizes energy, spirit, dynamism, and existence. In mythology, the birth of consciousness is associated with flame—and in many ways, our humanity is defined by our ability to produce, manipulate, and manage fire. But not all fires can be controlled. Fire is a primal force that offers warmth, light, and protection, along with destruction and devastation. Associated with the zodiac signs Aries, Leo, and Sagittarius, the Fire element speaks to courage, confidence, and curiosity. As the entire zodiac exists within you, consider how you can tap into the Fire energy in your life. What lights you up? What ignites you on a soul level? How do you evoke passion from smoldering rubble? How does your genius spark?

170

In European folklore, *familiars* were the name for witches' animal companions. These mystical allies—envoys of the otherworldly realms—emerge as intermediaries between the tangible and the ethereal. What truly distinguishes these spectral companions is the symbiotic bond they forge with their human counterparts. This relationship, created between metaphysical realms, yields a profound alchemy. It's a dynamic kinship, a harmonious symphony between worlds—a two-way channel of insight and intuition that transcends mere verbal or corporeal communication. Today, consider the familiars you've been blessed to know throughout your life: the cats or dogs that cohabit your space, birds that circulate your neighborhood, or even pesky rodents that have raided your kitchen. Each creature has a distinctive message and story to share. Today, reflect on what lessons and magic you've learned from your familiars.

Your garden is always in bloom. Let it flourish.

Prentis Hemphill—teacher, writer, embodiment coach—has an incredible quote, which I reflect on often: "Boundaries are the distance at which I can love you and me simultaneously." Boundaries are not cruel. They're not mean. They're not harsh or unkind. Boundaries are a form of respect; they enable us to live, love, and thrive in healthy, sustainable ways. When we set boundaries, we clarify our expectations and establish thoughtful awareness. Like an elegant fence guarding a precious garden, boundaries protect your inner landscape and nurture your well-being. Today, reflect on the areas in your life where boundaries may need fortification. Whether it's in relationships, work, or personal time, identify where your energy may be dissipating without reciprocity. Or where you're beginning to feel excessively fatigued, resentful, overworked, or are simply craving a necessary change. What boundaries do you need to establish? Where do they need to be implemented? And how will you express these important parameters? Setting boundaries isn't always easy, but when you do, you'll experience a profound transformation. Boundaries enable you to foster authentic connections and support the growth of genuine and meaningful relationships. Right now, give yourself permission to tend to yourself like the precious garden that you are, letting the vibrant blossoms of your well-being flourish in the rich, fertile soil of self-love.

One of the most elusive cards in the tarot is the Hanged Man, which depicts an individual who is quite literally upside down. The central figure dangles from a beam, one leg wrapped in rope and the other crossed around him, with his hands behind his back, presumably tied as well. While this sounds like a horrifically uncomfortable pose, a halo emanates from his head, symbolizing a connection to the Divine. His body is relaxed, at ease, and the expression on his face exudes a similar comfort. What an interesting paradox, to be flipped upside down and bound while also notably content. Likewise, the Hanged Man speaks to a moment or situation where we can't really take any steps forward, but we're all the better for it. The Hanged Man symbolizes pause, reflection, liminal space. It encourages us to approach our reality from a totally different perspective—perhaps even a 180-degree shift. The Hanged Man supports passive—as opposed to active—participation, reminding us that we don't always need to move full steam ahead. Right now, consider how you may be in need of the lessons of this tarot card.

Some people will exist in your narrative for a lifetime, a decade, a season, or a moment. All these connections are divinely guided—each one offers a unique gift. Perhaps it's patience, impermanence, or loyalty. Maybe it's boundaries, trust, or strength. Find gratitude for everyone and anyone who crosses your path: No matter how long your souls travel together, you received invaluable lessons that wouldn't have been possible without their influence.

Today, write a little poem for yourself. It doesn't need to be polished or precise. It can certainly be far from perfect. Maybe it will rhyme—maybe it won't. But right now, take a few moments to put thoughts on paper (or on your phone, whatever is most accessible). String ideas together like beads on a friendship bracelet. Let words sit, side-by-side, and observe their push and pull. Experiment with speed. Explore pauses, the flow of motion and stillness. Write a little poem and simply see where it goes.

Don't make yourself smaller to be convenient to others. Take up space.

In the Page of Pentacles, we meet an individual who's contemplating a shiny gold coin, which they hold in their hands. Standing in front of a bucolic backdrop, this individual is imagining auspicious future opportunities. Indeed, this card is associated with manifestation, hopes, dreams, wishes, and abundance. Right now, give yourself permission to imagine new financial opportunities that may unexpectedly come into your life. What do those look like? What do they feel like? How can you connect with these fantasies, giving yourself permission to feel the possibility on a cellular level? Think of this as a glass-half-full opportunity. What does it take to imagine a life with more prosperity, rewards, and unencumbered potential?

178

Don't speculate, communicate. Sometimes this is easier said than done. Seeking clarification, asking where someone stands on a topic, or following up with questions can be intimidating. Perhaps we're afraid of the answer—maybe we feel vulnerable in our query—or perhaps it should seem obvious and our asking the question would make us appear foolish. There are infinite reasons why we may feel shy about speaking up and engaging in dialogue. But when we speculate and infer an answer, we do a disservice to ourselves. We process the encounter only through our past experiences: what our psyche knows, understands, and has a foundation for comprehending. By seeking explanation, however, we present ourselves with the opportunity to learn. Today, consider where you can seek further knowledge and observe how that process makes you feel—both before and after. Your ability to courageously step into dialogue will guide you on your path.

Today, you're invited to give life to an intention using candle magic. You'll need a candle, a carving tool (you can use a pencil or pen, as well), oil (if you don't have scented oil, a cooking oil—such as olive oil or sunflower oil—can do the trick), herbs and/or spice (such as cinnamon, sugar, rosemary, or sage), and honey. First, set your intention. Do you want to attract love? Abundance? Opportunities? Peace? Happiness? Once you've established your desire, carve your will into your candle using a combination of symbols, words, and/or numbers—whatever you wish. Once you finish carving, lather your candle with oil and sprinkle it with herbs. Drizzle the top with honey to symbolize your benevolent intentions to the Universe, then light the candle. If you need to blow it out (before bed or leaving your home), simply say "thank you" each time you extinguish and reignite the flame.

In the Knight of Pentacles, we see an armored knight seated on a horse. There is no movement in this image as the knight sits calmly on his saddle, focused on the large, shiny gold coin held in his hands. Accordingly, this card is not about speedy, reactive, get-rich-quick schemes, but rather slow and steady success. It represents hard work, focus, and perseverance. It's keeping your attention on the long game, on building something sustainable that is truly meant to last. Today, think of how you can embody the Knight of Pentacles' thoughtful and methodical energy. When it comes to reaching your goals of abundance, what does patience and perseverance look like? What does it mean to be responsible, to make wise decisions, to thoughtfully navigate next steps? Consider how this approach plays out very differently than when we gamble, indulge in big risks, and expect instant results.

Today, you're invited to embody self-love by creating a potion. You'll need a cup (preferably one that's special to you), your favorite beverage (it could be anything!), a candle, a journal, and a pen. First, find a place in your home where you can spend a few minutes uninterrupted. Then light your candle, take a few deep breaths, and feel the weight of your body anchoring you to the earth. Pick up your pen, open your journal, and start freewriting about what self-love means to you. How can you fill your *proverbial* cup with strength, courage, compassion, and reverence? Tune in to your inner child—what kind of support did they need? How can you give them that love now? Once you're finished journaling, pour your beverage into your cup and read your words into the vessel. After you've infused it with your kind, compassionate magic, lift the cup and drink the beverage, absorbing all the positive blessings, inviting them to soak into your psyche.

Do you know what separates life from death? It's breath. Breath is the distinguishing feature of being alive. It's our ability to move the elements through our body, pump oxygen into our organs, and feel the vitality and electricity of existence as an inhale and exhale. Breath is life. When we are stressed, tense, or in a challenged state, we tend to obstruct our breath. We hold it. We limit it. We work against it. Today, I invite you to deepen your breath. Bring awareness to where the air fills your body. Your breath is profound, dynamic. It's your guide that keeps you moving, flowing, laughing, and loving. Treat your breath with reverence. Express gratitude for every inhale and exhale.

The Earth element is stable, solid, and tangible. It symbolizes materiality, structure, and real, concrete truth. Earth is everything that exists aboveground: the trees, the vines, the forest's abundant flora and fauna—as well as all that dwells beneath the surface: the soil, the roots, the mycelium. Earth is divine engineering; it's the landscapes that nurture on both physical and spiritual levels. Associated with the zodiac signs Taurus, Virgo, and Capricorn, the Earth element speaks to presence, precision, and purpose. As the entire zodiac exists within you, consider how you can tap into the Earth energy in your life. What do you need to feel stable? How do you branch out while remaining solidly rooted? What systems can you rely on? What does it mean to be supported on a soul level?

184

If we're going, going, *going* all the time, demanding more and more and *more*, setting intentions, calling out desires, making wishes, and constantly looking toward the future, then we are truly missing the experience of living. This existence is not just about accumulation—it's about moments. It's about presence. It's about our ability to find ourselves rooted, grounded, situated exactly where we are. Could things always be better? Could things feel more aligned? Could we acquire even richer abundance? Sure. But if we focus on all the ways that we are not currently where we want to be, then we lose sight of all the blessings, miracles, joys, and auspicious synchronicities that have brought us to where we are right now. We must resist the urge to only look forward without appreciating our ability to stand still. We must resist the introduction of late-stage capitalism into our magical practices. We must remember that gratitude is in and of itself a radical gesture. We must be willing to find peace with enough.

Wisdom won't compete with the cacophony of chaos.

Wisdom is patiently waiting for you in stillness.

When you receive ideas, insight, wisdom, or artistic inspiration, you are operating as a channel. You are a conduit for a higher force. When we enter a flow state, we can feel that energetic input moving through us, animating the cells in our body, transferring information, and guiding us to meaning. We can't always access this flow state, but today, consider what environments help foster that incredible connection to a higher identity. Are you someone who needs total isolation, complete quiet, and no distractions to get to this state of mind, or do you need to be around activity or buzz? There's no right or wrong. There is no hierarchy. Simply consider what environment suits you best, and support your ability to receive brilliant, inspired messaging from source itself.

In the Queen of Pentacles, Her Highness sits on a throne decorated with carvings of fruit, trees, angels, animals, and other symbols of abundance. She's situated in a bountiful garden framed by roses and vines—a clear connection to the material world. As the Queen of Pentacles looks down at the large gold coin she holds in her hands, she evokes a sense of quiet confidence. This card is about feeling protected, safe, and stable within your environment. While of course having all the lavish benefits of abundant resources is fantastic, the grounded and earthy nature of this tarot card reminds us that true prosperity starts from within. It originates from a feeling of personal safety and security. Today, consider what that means for you. How do you support your own protection? Your own peace? Your own sense of anchoring, groundedness, and deep foundation? If this is challenging, consider ways you can enhance your alignment with your *physical* body, in the *physical* world, in this *physical* moment—right now. You are here.

188

When things feel foggy, consider slowing down. Perhaps, right now, not everything is how it appears. Some parts of your path may be hidden—and that's okay. Sometimes, too much information at once can be overwhelming. Sometimes, it's better to receive wisdom incrementally. So, when things feel foggy, lean in to your patience and intuitive discernment. Trust your instincts. Rely on your inner guidance. Perhaps this is an opportunity to explore undiscovered aspects of your identity—the parts of you that simply *couldn't* be revealed when you're moving too fast. Let the fog and ambiguity gently rock you into introspection and reflective exploration. When things feel foggy, take your time.

Today, you're invited to perform a ritual to release whatever is holding you back. Grab a journal, pen, paper, scissors, and string. First, journal for several minutes on what you'd like to cut out of your life. It could be a toxic relationship, self-limiting belief, intrusive thought, etc. Once you've identified the connection you need to sever, tear or cut your paper in half. On one half of your paper, write in big, bold letters what you're purging. On the other half of your paper, write your name. Next, cut a small hole in both pieces of paper, feeding string into each half, connecting the two pieces of paper. Now, it's time to cut the cord. As you cut, recite: "I cut the cord that binds me. This cord was never mine. Heal in light and kindness 'til the end of time."

Respect what
you already have.

The King of Pentacles sits on his throne, so consumed by flora and fauna that the boundaries between robe, body, and the ground become indistinguishable. In one hand, he holds a scepter, and in the other, a large, shiny gold coin. The incredible amount of fabric, texture, and tapestry in this card illuminates its deep connection to the material world. The King of Pentacles is wealthy. There is an ease, comfort, and confidence in his stature, as well as a clear connection to his physical environment. While one can certainly fear becoming too consumed by the material world, especially as the lines between illustrated objects are blurred, this card reminds us that we can achieve the type of abundance and prosperity we hope to manifest. We can give ourselves permission to dream big, to think expansively, to recognize the extraordinary potential that motivates direction. Today, give yourself permission to imagine this realm of material comforts fully and unapologetically. Remember that money is an energetic frequency. By tapping into receiving, you also move with the vibration of giving. So, perhaps as an exercise, consider supporting a person or organization that touches your heart through a generous donation. Energy flows where intention goes.

Today, consider what it means for you to lead with curiosity. To explore, learn, wonder, listen. If something's not for you, that's fine! But maybe your perspective can be a gentle one—one that's anchored in empathy and compassion. Maybe you can find a new way of learning. Or unlearning. Or investigating skepticism. Or fear. Or doubt. Maybe your curiosity can generate breakthroughs that are wider and richer and more expansive than you ever imagined possible. Maybe your curiosity is a connection to the Divine.

Of course, it's easier to follow the rules, do the things that everyone else is doing, find stability in the conventional, prescriptive path, and not use your imagination, ingenuity, or unique sensibilities. It's tempting to conform. To adapt. To comply. But . . . then what? What will happen when your soul rejects these shackles? When your soul needs to express the unique, thorny sides and oblong contours of your spirit that don't fit neatly into a prefabricated box? What will happen when the milestones, the accolades, and all the silly standards of status quo "success" no longer fulfill you? What will happen then? Because—at a certain point—following the rules will eventually lead to a dead end. So today, consider the ways that you can break them—just a little! Gently enough to not disrupt your whole life. Take back your individuality and do things your way. Don't be afraid to write your own story.

The Death card may seem intimidating. After all, it depicts a skeleton riding on a white horse, with a motionless corpse on the ground beneath the animal's hooves. But this card is not about physical death. It's about rebirth—emotional metamorphosis. In the background of this image, the sun rises at dawn, casting bright rays across the horizon—a symbol of new beginning, opportunities, stories, and life. The Death card reveals that, in order to access the promise of tomorrow, we must be willing to release our psychological shackles. We must be willing to—bravely and courageously—step forward. We must be willing to face our emotional carnage and confront painful past experiences. Today, consider what you need to let go of in order to begin again. What does rebirth, resurrection, and renewal mean to you? How can you incorporate the lessons of the Death card into your current circumstances? In the metaphysical world, death isn't finality; it's just a redirection within the cosmic spiral.

You create as you speak—
this is the meaning of
the ancient, alchemical
word *abracadabra*.

Today's journey invites you to savor the magic of mindful eating, a practice that nourishes not only your body but also your soul. Just as a chef crafts a masterpiece with intention, you *can* transform your meals into moments of profound presence and gratitude. Prepare a simple, nourishing meal or snack, and set aside a quiet space for dining. Eliminate distractions, silence your phone, and create an atmosphere of serenity. As you sit down to eat, take a few deep breaths to center yourself. Engage your senses fully in the experience. Notice the colors, textures, and aromas of your food. As you take your first bite, pay attention to the flavors and the sensation of each morsel. Chew slowly and savor the experience. Allow your meal to become a meditation—a sacred moment of connection between you and the nourishing gifts of the Divine. How does mindful eating make you feel? Do you notice a greater sense of satisfaction and awareness? Carry this practice with you, recognizing that every meal can be an opportunity for presence, nourishing every aspect of your being.

The Air element is malleable, adaptable, and ever-present. It symbolizes thoughts, ideas, words, and connections. In ancient traditions, air represented the invisible fortress that separated earth from sky, dutifully bolstering the heavens so it didn't come crashing down on the physical plane. But air is also a powerful conductor, responsible for transmitting whispers, messages, and signals. Associated with the zodiac signs Gemini, Libra, and Aquarius, the Air element speaks to friendship, partnership, and humanitarianism. As the entire zodiac exists within you, consider how you can tap into the Air energy in your life. What does it mean to express yourself? How do you share, receive, and process information? What does connection mean to you? How does your imagination fortify your soul?

198

Life grows in the most unexpected places. Dandelions sprout from cracks in the sidewalk. Moss consumes grouting. Ragweed busts through floorboards. And you're growing, not in spite of but *because* of your circumstances. Your roots are getting stronger, denser, more resilient. Don't stop now.

Energy flows
where intention goes.

In the mystical world, opposites are the same. A full moon, for instance, occurs when the Sun and Moon meet at 180 degrees in the sky, flowing across the same axis. Although the two signs on either side of this axis have different ways of reaching a shared perspective, fundamentally, there is an intrinsic agreement as to how these mystical energies express themselves. So, when you find yourself vehemently opposed to something, it may be worth considering whether your state of mind is not that different from what you are rejecting. When we play in the world of opposition, we recognize that there are always two sides to the same coin, that darkness and light exist within the same spectrum, that polarities are really one and the same. Right now, consider how opposites illuminate your psyche and what these opposing perspectives mean to you.

The Ace of Swords depicts a hand—emerging from a cloud—holding a sword pointed upright. A crown, draped by a victory wreath, is perched at the tip of the sword, alluding to auspicious possibilities. The Ace of Swords symbolizes raw, unadulterated ideas. It represents new thoughts, new ways of seeing the world, new perspectives on reality. In tarot, the Swords suit symbolizes the mind, cognition, thoughts, the way we process information, and our mental faculties. Accordingly, the Ace of Swords invites us to tap into spaces of genius, breakthroughs, innovation. What ideas are you currently exploring? Maybe it's a twinkle at first—a glimmer of a notion—so give yourself permission to expand this inkling. Follow it. Investigate it. Nurture it. Tap into your curiosity to see where this ideation may lead. Just let your mind wander.

Sometimes the Universe wants you to speak. It wants you to articulate your needs, your desires, your curiosities. And other times, the Universe wants you to listen. It wants you to observe. It wants you to take in the frequencies around you, the aromas in the air, the way the sun passes through leaves, and the different sounds birds make in their calls. Sometimes the Universe wants to give you direction in the form of embraces, lessons, or symbols. Sometimes the Universe knows better than we can ever even begin to comprehend, and its divine wisdom arrives in both grand and subtle ways, which means it's our responsibility to pay attention to everything.

203

Today, journey into the sanctuary of your dreams, a realm where your subconscious mind weaves stories, messages, and symbols. Like an ancient oracle, your dreams offer insights into your inner world, guiding you toward self-discovery and transformation. Before you go to sleep, set an intention to remember your dreams. When you wake in the morning, write down what you remember in a journal. Consider the emotions they stirred, the questions they raised, or the guidance they offered. Your dreams may reveal hidden desires, unresolved issues, or insights into your personal journey. As you delve into the recesses of your psyche, remember that they're a profound source of healing. By honoring and exploring your dreams, you open a door to the depths of your subconscious mind, where the wisdom of your inner self resides. Embrace this nightly adventure as a sacred ritual of self-exploration. In the realm of dreams, you're both the dreamer and the interpreter, journeying into the mysteries of your soul.

Let your grief waltz
with love—they are,
ultimately, one and the same.

The Two of Swords is set at dusk, as indicated by the moody grayish-blue sky and the crescent moon that shines overhead in front of a tranquil, bucolic lake. Our central figure sits on a stool, blindfolded, with their arms crossed, each displaying a sword. This person is on guard, defenses up—yet they appear to be safe. Perhaps they don't know that there is no imminent danger? That all is calm? Likewise, this card reminds us that anxiety, fear, and past challenging experiences can get in the way of our ability to be present and recognize the unique variables of our current situation. While we certainly don't want to be naive—and it's important to maintain discretion—the Two of Swords indicates an inability to truly understand our current conditions. Right now, think about how that might relate to your life. Are you projecting fear, disappointment, and sadness from the past onto your current moment? If so, consider lowering your shield—maybe you *can* trust the Universe, after all.

If you're waiting for things to change, the first place you should look is your internal narrative. What are you saying to yourself? What are the types of words, conversations, and dialogues happening within your psyche? Your internal narrative is either going to block your blessings or welcome them with open arms. You're going to either be receptive to the miracles, the abundance, the magic, and the alchemy—or you're going to deny, reject, and return these offerings to sender. If you're waiting for something to change, before you point fingers externally, take a moment to consider what storyline is unfolding within.

Crystals are dazzling. They glisten, reflect, and radiate stunning, prismatic colors. It's no wonder we incorporate these majestic items into our spiritual practices. But stones don't need to exude kaleidoscopic qualities to be enchanted. Stones—the shades of gray pebbles we encounter every day—are suspiciously ordinary. And, like all organic matter on this planet, stones are sentient. Stones emit energy. Stones carry a powerful life-force. Our ancestors knew this; they were, of course, aware of the consciousness baked into these fragments of earth. Think back to your childhood: whether you were collecting them at the beach or in your own backyard, you were aware of their power, too. You were drawn to their magnetism. Stones are the earth's formidable bones, and as we call upon this primordial foundation, we're reminded of our soul's own everlasting core. Stones symbolize eternity, illuminating our incredible resilience and connection to what is permanent, solid, and ancient. Stones are the links between our ephemeral world and the soul's enduring journey. So today, I invite you to pick up the most ordinary stone you can find, hold it in your palm, and consider your soul's own everlasting magic.

The Three of Swords is one of the most iconic images in tarot. This card features a classic, stylized red heart punctured by three long swords stabbing it vertically and diagonally. Behind the heart is a storm; rain pours down from thick, gray clouds. Simply put, this card is heartbreak. It's sorrow. It's the experience of loss, grief, hurt. This card is an homage to the pain that we we've all experienced at some point in our lives—rejection, disappointment, heartache. This card reminds us that we are in a constant state of healing. That mending and tending to our wounds is an incredibly important part of our spiritual journey. We cannot avoid sadness, nor should we, as it is such a magnificently human emotion. If we recognize that sorrow is an inevitable truth, then right now, consider all the ways that you support your own tender healing.

Find the spark
in your heart and
fan your flame.

Today, you're invited to explore how you can show up as your beautiful, truthful, authentic self within relationships and larger communities. It may seem straightforward, but consider all the ways you might be adjusting how you speak, dress, offer—or don't offer—your opinions to accommodate others. Existing authentically is an incredibly vulnerable act, so right now, consider what it means for you to tap into your unabashed bravery. What does it look like to be fully you? How can you contribute to your relationships and communities while also honoring your amazing, nuanced, complex self? We've all inherited or internalized expectations from our parents, extended families, cultures, and societies. Right now, your invitation is to recognize which patterns serve you and which don't. Let this awareness reignite your inner strength so that you can better embody and express your innate identity. That's your truth. That's your soul. Baby, that's you.

211

The Water element is fluid, deep, and spirited. It symbolizes emotions, intuition, surrender, and clairvoyance. There's always been an inextricable link between water and psyche: the ocean's impenetrable depth is akin to the incomprehensible scope of the subconscious. And just as different types of water exist—shallow, murky, fresh, choppy—so do different varieties of feelings and states of being. Associated with the zodiac signs Cancer, Scorpio, and Pisces, the Water element speaks to sensitivity, intensity, and mysticism. As the entire zodiac exists within you, consider how you can tap into the Water energy in your life. How do you process your emotions? How do your senses illuminate your intuition? In which ways does your divine wisdom light your way? How does your internal world mirror your soul's authentic truth?

212

Love, of any kind, must be rooted in confidence. Empowerment. Justice. Authenticity. Compromising yourself isn't love—it's loss. We cannot love others if we don't know how to love ourselves, and that means loving ourselves as the imperfect, chronically incomplete beings that we are. Loving ourselves not *in spite of* our perceived flaws but *because* of those oblong blemishes and oddities that define our character. That's the foundation of true devotional, radical acceptance. Loving the enemy within.

Attachment isn't connection; attachment is projection.

214

You're here for a reason. Some days, you'll feel extremely in touch with your purpose. Other days, the method to the madness feels vague, opaque, ambiguous, and uncertain—and that's absolutely fine. You're not always supposed to understand the bigger spiritual rationale behind your existence. In a way, you never will because the story of your soul is so much greater, richer, wiser, and wider than what you can comprehend on a day-to-day basis. It takes time. It takes years. It takes decades to unpack the extraordinary potential that you have incarnated in this lifetime. Across many lifetimes. So this isn't something you need to figure out right now. This isn't something you need to solve today or tomorrow or even within the next year. This is something you will need to inhale. This is an atmosphere. This is an attitude. This is a way of moving through the world and confidently knowing that you're here for a reason, even if you don't know why.

The Four of Swords shows us a knight lying horizontally on a sarcophagus, although it appears his form has been built into the tomb itself. Beneath his horizontal body lies a single sword, while three swords are displayed above him. The Four of Swords speaks to rest, meditation, contemplation, and recuperation. It invites us to find stillness and pause, to turn off to the world—at least temporarily. In a way, this card evokes the essence of the Savasana or Corpse pose in yoga: a simulation of death that clears our mind and grounds our body. Have you been giving yourself time to rest and recover? Are you fully embodied—or have you been frantically moving through your day-to-day in autopilot? Right now, consider pressing pause and giving yourself a well-deserved break.

216

For better or for worse, we're byproducts of our habits: the time we wake up, the food we eat, the type of content we consume. So today, I encourage you to be mindful about what you're doing, on an hour-by-hour basis. This type of awareness can feel harsh or critical, but this exercise isn't about judging yourself; it's about observing. It's about recognizing what you're taking in and how that stimuli shapes your broader experience. Today, I want you to consider the ways your ideas, perceptions, and philosophies are a direct reaction to the tiny choices that accumulate, defining your experience at large. If you're looking to make a big change, perhaps minor adjustments to your schedule will yield cataclysmic results.

Sacred geometry speaks to the patterns, shapes, and cycles that exist within the natural world. It's the coils of a fingerprint and the rings of a tree. It's seashells and galaxies, hurricanes and Fibonacci sequences. It's the star at the center of an apple and the invisible pentagram formed by Venus's distinctive orbit. More broadly, sacred geometry urges us to pay attention to the systems that shape our reality, both within the physical and metaphysical realms. At its core, sacred geometry emphasizes the idea that everything in existence is connected through divine proportions and harmonious designs. It prompts us to recognize the inherent beauty in the symmetries that govern life, a reminder that we're all playing an essential role in this beautiful cosmic dance. Today, consider how your choices—both conscious and subconscious—reflect patterns, shapes, and cycles that permeate your existence. What do they mean? What do they tell you? And how do they reflect your personal relationship with magic?

When the Sun and Moon are in the same sign, the Moon is in its new moon phase. During this period, there is no nocturnal illumination—the sky is at its absolute darkest. In the wild, it's easiest to hide from nighttime predators during this time, which means our ancient ancestors utilized the new moon to nest, reflect, and dream up new ideas. They didn't need to be on guard, so this stage offered a rare opportunity to find calm. Today, we utilize the new moon (the beginning of the lunar cycle) to set intentions, plant seeds, and manifest change. No matter where you are in the current lunar cycle, consider how the energy of this phase—the poetic combination of safety and creativity—shows up in your life.

In the Five of Swords, we see a sly-looking individual picking up three swords from the ground. Glancing over their shoulder, this person observes two other individuals who are walking away, expressing sadness and despair. One appears to be crying, covering their face with their hands. Two additional swords lie on the ground, and the sky is punctuated with dark gray, angular clouds, symbolizing tension and uneasiness. This scene shows the aftermath of a conflict. It depicts defeat, surrender, disagreements, and even deception. It reminds us that we must choose our battles wisely—not every fight is worth the consequences. Today, consider whether you've been directing attention to something or someone who has been depleting your energy. Perhaps, rather than engaging in constant discord, this is an opportunity to move toward acceptance, recognizing that people have different wants, needs, and expectations. Not every situation is going to be ideal. Acknowledging the limitations of our circumstances is not the same as giving up. It's being strategic, empowering us to reclaim our agency as we direct focus to the things that really matter.

220

Boundaries are a symbol of balance—they enable us to stabilize different perspectives. Compromise is the key to all successful relationships, and some dynamics require more clarification than others. Today, I invite you to consider the harmony and symmetry—as well as the negotiations and sacrifices—you make within your own bonds. Are your interpersonal relationships fair and just? Even if you're not completely satisfied with the (explicit or implicit) agreements, is there an evenly distributed give-and-take? Right now, give yourself permission to examine and reexamine the terms and conditions of your relationships—romantic, platonic, and professional. What's working? What isn't? What needs to be updated or reworked altogether? Remember, all contracts are negotiable. Don't let anyone tell you otherwise.

It's fine to want it all—I want you to want it all!—but we can't have it all . . . all at once. If your magic is too scattered and too broad, it's going to be difficult to track your progress. So, with each spell or ritual you perform, focus on a very specific intention. For example, you don't need to manifest both a new romantic partner and a promotion at the same moment. Just choose one at a time. You will have plenty of opportunities to expand your practice to call upon all the exciting wishes your heart desires. After all, manifestation is a marathon, not a sprint.

In the Six of Swords, we see a woman (obscured by a cape) and a young child being ferried across a body of water to nearby land. The figures' backs are to us so we cannot make out their identities, but their body language shows loss or sorrow as their heads hang low. Seven swords are propped up vertically in the boat. On the right side, turbulent water indicates a difficult time, while the sea ahead is calm and tranquil, symbolizing a movement toward more peaceful conditions. There is anonymity in this card, as all the figures remain somewhat mysterious. We can infer that this scene is an escape, that these individuals are leaving quietly and covertly. They are—perhaps—getting out unscathed. Likewise, this reminds us that we are always allowed to leave—and when we do, we may feel empowered and protected in our exit. Although nobody wants to have to pack up and start anew, there is opportunity and potential filled with new ideas and fresh energy that will empower us to begin again. The Six of Swords invites us to make our exit, and consider what may be in our best interest to leave behind.

What a privilege to surrender and trust that, at the end of the day, everything will work out. Because why shouldn't it?

224

When I was young, a relative told me that if I don't love the process, I should quit while I'm ahead. That if I'm only focused on the outcome or the product, I'm not fully prepared for the journey. This idea haunted me for years, especially because, broadly speaking, I'm not a huge fan of process. I don't like mundane, repetitive tasks. I get annoyed by needing to invest time, energy, and resources without seeing a return. As I've gotten older and continued to contemplate this relative's point of view, I don't think it's accurate. There are certain instances, yes, when the process defines the outcome, when *doing and becoming* are so inextricably linked and you cannot separate one from the other. But there are also times when the process is a means to an end, when the steps just help you arrive at your destination. Not every road is going to be the scenic route. Sometimes you just need to move forward to push toward the goal. So right now, if you're feeling discouraged by your endless to-do list, your thankless job, or all of the tedious tasks that feel daunting, don't lose sight of the bigger picture. Don't give up on your beautiful, expansive vision. You don't need to love every step of the way. Sometimes, just getting through is good enough.

During the waxing crescent phase, which is the second phase of the lunar cycle, the Moon appears as a thin sliver, the smallest slice just barely visible against the darkness of the night sky. There is an anticipatory nature to this time; the Moon is growing, both in size and confidence. As the Moon symbolizes our inner world, this signals an exciting emotional shift, indicating the beginning of new possibilities. As we push through the darkness, we move past complacency and are inspired to act. No matter where you are in the current lunar cycle, consider how the energy of this phase—eagerness and motivation—shows up in your life.

Today, I invite you to turn the most ordinary place in your home—maybe your bedroom, kitchen, or bathroom—into a sacred sanctuary. Perhaps you imagine that cleaning this environment clears space in your psyche, or maybe it symbolizes recommitting yourself to your spiritual practice. Spend some time throwing out old mail, tidying surfaces, and creating a sense of balance and harmony through organization. Once you've finished, center yourself in the middle of the room. Take three deep breaths to settle your energy and tap into your intuition. Now that you've created new pathways for energy, what mystical messages are you receiving?

What did you learn from your last spiritual breakthrough?

We are constantly collaborating. These partnerships may not be defined through contracts or agreements, but life is always a give-and-take. We are processing, reacting, responding, initiating, anticipating. Today, consider your most inspired collaborators. Perhaps it's your best friend from childhood, your significant other, or the person who works at your local deli. Perhaps it's a memory of a teacher who challenged you to be the best version of yourself. Right now, take a moment to honor these collaborators. Send them your appreciation and thanks. This could be something you do through a phone call, a text message, a visit, or quietly through the etheral astral plane. Put your hand to your heart, bow your head down, and acknowledge appreciation for the collaborators who have helped illuminate your path forward.

229

In the Seven of Swords, a suspicious-looking individual tiptoes away from a carnival carrying five swords—as many as they can hold. Why is this person sneaking away? What business do they have carrying those swords—where are they going with them? This card speaks to deception, manipulation, and trickery. While we, of course, always want to think of others as benevolent, the truth is that not everyone has pure intentions. There are ulterior motives or—at the very least—conflicting agendas that may cause conflict with our own trajectory. Right now, be very discerning. Who are you taking advice from? What are their credentials? How can you be sure that they are truly trustworthy? Alternatively, this card may reveal your own sneaky behavior. If that's the case, remember that the Universe does not favor deception. At the end of the day, honesty and courage are always rewarded. Make sure you are genuine and authentic with both your words and actions.

230

When we think of setting intentions or performing manifestation magic, we often go straight for the biggest, most elaborate visions we can muster. And, oftentimes, these big aspirations end up resembling the over-the-top, excess-dominated culture we see reflected (and sanctified) across media. Money. Fame. Houses. Designers. Luxury. Over the years, I've seen so many people set "goals" for concepts that mirror the "aspirational" lifestyles that consume our digital timelines. And, naturally, this makes me wonder whether we really want these things . . . or if it's the byproduct of being brainwashed by a society obsessed with billionaires? Today, challenge yourself to explore your wants, needs, and desires that exist beyond consumerism. What things speak to your soul that don't involve money or status? What expressions of your true self light you up, independently from others' approval? Today, focus on nothing fancy. Let raw simplicity be your guide.

We mystics know that time isn't linear—all time is happening at the same time... all the time. But, as mere mortals, we do experience life chronologically, which means we move through a past, present, and future. Today, write three letters to these different expressions of yourself at these distinctive moments in time. For each letter, set a timer for a short duration (three or four minutes per letter) and let your psyche take over. What does your younger self need to know? What guidance can you offer yourself in the present? And, finally, what extraordinary wisdom will your future self share? By exploring all the different dimensions of time and identity, you're connecting with the full expression of your soul, honoring all the versions of your reality that are—even still—happening in tandem. That's what we call portal magic.

If others reject you,
it's their loss. If you
reject you, you're lost.

The Temperance card defies the laws of physics. In this image, water is being poured upward, moving from the lower chalice to the higher chalice. The central figure—adorned in a sacred, esoteric robe—has giant avian wings sprouting from their back, and a glowing halo emanates from their head, signaling a connection to the Divine. This card is about enlightenment, healing, and a powerful connection to magic, alchemy, and our ability to transform situations. For us to do this, we need to bring balance, patience, and moderation into the equation. This card speaks to sobriety, to clear thoughts and a clear mind. It advises against extremes and encourages us to find harmony in our ability to alchemize multiple elements simultaneously. There is a quiet confidence to this card: the ability to open our heart to faith and possibilities by way of our own channeled healing. Indeed, this card has a powerful connection to rehabilitation and recovery. So today, consider what your own healing journey looks like and how you can tap into those lessons—how you've changed, grown, and healed over time to make magic in your life.

234

Life is long and meandering, filled with many experiences, stages, and happenings. But somewhere—within the vast expanse of your psyche—you remember that moment playing in the sun, what it feels like to walk into your elementary school classroom, that conversation with your best friend when you were nine years old. Somewhere, buried in your memories, you can recall your first crush, your first taste of independence, your first disappointment, first heartbreak, first chilly day. Somehow everything is stored within the beautiful architecture of your consciousness. All it takes is the slightest amount of stimulation to awaken these distant, seemingly forgotten moments. Right now, find one of these memories and let it take up space at the front of your psyche. What does it feel like? Where does it live in your body, and what can it tell you about right now? Explore it with curiosity.

Two parameters I incorporate into my journaling practice are prompts and time restraints—and I often use them together. Today, grab a pen and paper, and take 10 minutes to experiment with purposeful journaling. Ask yourself three questions: What inspires my art? What's my unique voice? How does my story uplift others? For each of these, give yourself three minutes (per prompt) to write as much as you can. Let the words flow, keep your pen moving. If you get stuck, you can jot that down ("I don't know what to write"), but maintain connection with the page. Through prompts and time restraints, you'll give yourself permission to explore complex topics without overthinking. You'll empower your psyche, your creativity, and your innate truth to speak fearlessly and unabashedly. Even better, you can use this technique whenever you're seeking soul-guided clarification.

The Eight of Swords depicts a person bound and blindfolded among eight swords vertically anchored in the ground. As swords are a symbol of the mind, cognition, and our own mental faculties, this scene symbolizes the way we become blocked and stifled by our own worries, anxieties, and limiting beliefs. This card is often interpreted as self-imposed restriction; feeling trapped by our circumstances and anxieties. Right now, consider whether your intrusive thoughts have gotten the better of you. What do you tell yourself when you look in the mirror? How do you greet yourself in the morning when you start your day? What kinds of words, statements, and ideologies inform your inner monologue? Today, consider how these statements could be affecting or impacting your movement forward. If you feel like nothing is shifting, give yourself permission to first change your mindset.

To generate abundance, visualize your aura—colorful and glittering—growing wider and brighter each time you step through a doorway. Your magnetism will attract opportunities beyond your wildest dreams.

When we begin to tap into our magic, it can feel foreign and intimidating. We might feel clumsy, like a toddler teetering on plump legs. When we adopt a new skill, we default back to our early days of academic learning, which says that there is a right and a wrong way. One is deserving of praise, the other of punishment. But this is not how magic works—there is no "right" and there is no "wrong." These tools are meant to empower you, uplift you, bring you back to a preverbal state where you're developing on a purely instinctual level. Unaware of standards, rubrics, or percentiles. Magic comes straight from the soul— the same soul that lifted you up on those tiny legs to take your first courageous steps. Magic cannot be used incorrectly. As long as your practice aligns with your intention, everything will be exactly as it should. So mote it be.

When the Moon reaches its first quarter, also known as the half moon phase, it arrives at 50 percent illumination. While one side of the Moon remains entirely in shadow, the other side is bright, vivid, and electrically charged. Symbolically, this reflects a powerful shift in perspective: Although we don't have access to the full story yet, we are continuing to grow, move toward our goals, and process information as it's being revealed. Likewise, this Moon is a time for planning and organizing; important changes are about to transpire. No matter where you are in the current lunar cycle, consider how the energy of this phase—awareness and activation—shows up in your life.

Vulnerability is not a means to an end. You aren't vulnerable to attract the right partner, cultivate deeper friendships, or unlock a certain "bragging right" within your self-actualization journey. Vulnerability is not a tool. It's not a strategy. And, if employ vulnerability a tool to yield rewards, is it really vulnerability in the first place, or is it something more dubious—a mechanism of the ego designed to achieve the praise? Vulnerability is raw, authentic, pure. Yes, it can help us create deeper and more meaningful relationships when it's experienced authentically. But the practice of becoming authentically vulnerable—as opposed to conveniently vulnerable—is one that requires deep soul work. It demands that we strip away the layers of ego, facade, and projection to truly connect with the deepest version of truth.

241

Today, you're invited to channel energy into your professional pursuits. Write a letter to the Universe about an opportunity and the compensation you want to receive, penning your words in the present tense—as if your intentions have already come to fruition (for example, "I have a job that makes me feel appreciated and respected," "I make a [certain amount of money] per week without compromising my work-life balance," or "I have the freedom to pick and choose projects that spark my creativity"). Be as specific as you can, describing how you feel, where you work, what you do, what your day-to-day looks like, and how much you're paid for your tasks. Fold up the letter and place it under a candle. Let the candle burn down completely. Every morning, reread the letter out loud until your wishes have been granted.

242

What would happen if you just took the pressure off? Would would happen if you laughed at yourself, had a little bit more fun, and embraced a more playful sensibility? This isn't about writing off your goals. Of course you're an important, meaningful, powerful person. The things you do, think, and create are worthy of reverence and acclaim—you are no joke. But all along the way, you can relinquish the heavy stoicism. The process of becoming your best, most self-actualized self can be a silly one. It can be weird. It can be jovial. It can be bright and buoyant, filled with delightful twists and turns. This journey doesn't need to be a solemn endeavor. Today, consider ways you can infuse your experience with a little more laughter, a little more childlike wonder, a little more humor, and a little more freedom.

243

In the Nine of Swords, we see a person sitting up in bed at night, hands covering their face. Their expression is of deep agony, perhaps having just been jolted awake by a terrible nightmare. Nine swords hang horizontal above them, and the quilt draped across their body depicts astrological symbols. This is a stressful, albeit relatable, moment: unable to sleep because of anxieties, worries, depression, fears, or intrusive thoughts. Today, think of whether this is something coming up in your life right now. Are you struggling to find calm due to high stress or unresolved narratives that are making you tense and worried? Is there something you've been obsessing over internally? If so, it's time to make a change. Communicate your concerns. Share what's on your mind. Speak to your trusted allies about what you're internally navigating, recognizing that the best way to move forward is by shining light on your stressful situations. Your mental health is important, and the Nine of Swords reminds us that speaking your truth aloud—in the waking hours—is always of the utmost importance.

244

Even on a cloudy day, the sun is still shining beneath the coverage. This is a metaphor for your own illumination, wisdom, and power. Not all days are going to be radiant and glowing. Not all days are going to give you the answers or fuel the drive and the vitality to move forward. Some days are gloomy, some are gray. Some are confusing, foggy, or simply sad. But even if you're experiencing this proverbial overcast sky, remember that on the other side of this dense cloud cover, there's still optimism, hope, and your radiant bright soul—just waiting for the next opportunity to exude warmth.

245

Today, you're invited to perform a ritual to release anything that's holding you back. You'll need a pen, paper, and salt. Take a few deep breaths and feel the weight of your body anchoring you to the earth. When you're ready, write all your blocks down on your piece of paper. As your hand moves, some obvious obstacles may rise to the surface—but let yourself go even deeper, unearthing the unexpected restrictions that are locked in the folds of your psyche. When you're finished, sprinkle salt in a circle around the paper; first counterclockwise, then clockwise. Let this paper sit enclosed in the salt circle for 24 hours—during this time, the salt (an extraordinary alchemical cleansing mineral) will dissolve the blocks. After the time has elapsed, dispose of the paper and salt, trusting that the spell has been spun.

May you have the courage
to know when it's time
to walk away.

The Ten of Swords illustrates a grisly scene. An individual is face down, presumably dead, with 10 swords stabbed into their back. The sky is dark and ominous, but in the distance, dawn begins to emerge on the horizon. The Ten of Swords symbolizes an ending, a completion, the final page in the book. It's not a literal death, of course, but rather a powerful line in the sand. What was once is now no longer—the inevitable moment of rebirth is upon us. What does this imagery and symbolism evoke for you? Are you on the precipice of a major ending? What does it mean to accept—fully and completely—when something has concluded? Although it is never easy to say good-bye, the Ten of Swords reminds us that acknowledging the space between an ending and a beginning is a critical part of the self-actualization journey. It's okay to let go.

248

I hope that you receive everything that you want and that unexpected blessings make their way to you. I hope that the energy of this sunrise to sunset sparkles within you, and you discover new possibilities that exceed your wildest imagination. But maybe that isn't going to be today. Maybe today is going to feel lackluster or disappointing. Maybe you'll be faced with some rejection, some misplaced frustration will find you. But today is just a passing, fleeting moment. Today is ephemeral. Today is not forever—and today is not everything. So whenever you find yourself having an annoying, frustrating, disappointing, or shitty day, don't turn that shitty day into a shitty week, that shitty week into a shitty month, and that shitty month into a shitty year. Nothing is permanent. Everything is fluid. Let today just be *today,* however it manifests. Let it sleep with sunset. And as you wake up and begin a new 24-hour cycle, let the opportunities and the possibilities renew, as well.

An altar is any surface that's used specifically to create connections to the spiritual world. Altars are often the centerpiece of a magical practice—it's a physical space that speaks directly to the astral dimensions. You can turn any area into an altar, so long as you're using material space and objects as a touchstone to the spiritual world. The first step in creating an altar is to choose its location. Tailor your altar to fit your environment and personal mystical practice. The size of your altar isn't important—it's your intention that infuses it with magic and purpose. If your space is on the smaller side, you may choose to create a portable altar, one that you can easily tuck away. If you have more room, you may choose to devote a table, windowsill, top of dresser, or corner to your altar. Next, gather objects (such as a decorative tablecloth) to delineate your sacred space: candles, incense or smudge, crystals, plants, herbs, pictures, etc. Arrange your objects on your altar and explore how this deepens your magical practice. Your sacred space is meant to evolve with you. Refreshing your altar on a consistent basis is a beautiful way to sustain a connection to the mystical realm, amplify your manifestations, and honor your self-actualization journey.

250

One of the most intriguing aspects of the notorious Devil card is that all of the figures depicted in the iconography have a choice—no one is trapped. The male and female characters are bound by a metal chain, with shackles around their necks. But these shackles are not tight; they're loose, signifying that these two individuals have bound themselves willingly to a situation. Accordingly, the Devil card speaks to the obsessions, fixations, and compulsions that we *actually* have agency over. It represents the recurring habits and behaviors that we might recognize as destructive, but in the moment feel good, enticing, or desirable. There is a strong link to addiction with this card, and the behaviors that we find ourselves repeating over and over again. Today, think about your obsessions and fixations. What are you bound to and what would it look like to loosen the shackles and free yourself from the confines of obsession?

Don't waste
this moment wishing
for another.

252

How often do you look in the mirror and decide you're not worthy enough? That you're not talented enough, that your ideas aren't original enough? That you're not smart enough? Wealthy enough? Organized enough? But what is this concept of *enough*? Who's measuring with tape? Who's grading the test? Who's codified this value system? Right now, recognize that you're holding yourself to standards that were made up by noxious forces—systems that were meant to oppress, constrict, and erase. Systems that have poisoned the well for so many generations that we can barely taste the toxins. But the disease continues to fester; it shows up in the concept of *enough*. So today, free your system of this pollutant. You are enough. You are whole. You are sacred.

During the waxing gibbous phase, the Moon is nearly full, reaching up to 99 percent illumination. This is a powerful expression of lunar emotional energy: Growing in both size and scale, the Moon becomes round and ripe, ready to burst into its next cycle. During this stage, we take our intentions to the next level by adding even more layers of dimensionality. We may begin to challenge, question, and ask why. There's an inherent curiosity baked into the waxing gibbous moon. No matter where you are in the current lunar cycle, consider how the energy of this phase—curiosity and momentum—shows up in your life.

254

Nourishment isn't just about good food, movement, and rest. Nourishment is about our community, the people we choose to spend time with, the ideas that stimulate our curiosity, and the pleasures that activate our soul. Nourishment is an openness, receptivity, and connection to alchemical changes, which blossom like seasons. Nourishment is a commitment to life.

Today, I invite you to tap into the frequency of abundance. For this ritual, you'll need a jar, plus any objects or herbs you associate with abundance—such as coins, photos, ticket stubs, dice, crystals, trinkets, and spices and flowers (like allspice, basil, bay leaves, cinnamon, star anise, cloves, dill, gardenia, lavender, or rose). On a piece of paper, write your definition of abundance and place it in the jar. Then add your objects and herbs one-by-one to your jar as you repeat your definition aloud. Seal the jar, hold it to your heart, and speak, "So mote it be." Connect with your jar every day by holding it to your heart or giving it a little shake while envisioning your intention. This will ensure the magic remains fresh and active.

To perceive is
to believe.

In the Page of Swords, we see our central character standing at the top of a hill on a windy day. A large gust blows back his hair. As he stands in an active position with his sword raised toward the sky, he channels a curious, present, dynamic spirit. In tarot, the Swords suit is associated with the mind, ideas, and cognition. Likewise, this card signifies an idea person. Perhaps that's you. Right now, consider whether you are embodying the Page of Swords. Do you have curiosities that are moving through you like wind? Do you have a clever, active mind that feels best in motion? There is a sense of adventure in the Page of Swords. Right now, reflect on what that might mean for you.

I know there are so many things you want to do and accomplish and achieve. Some of these goals might be hyper specific, connected to a certain time, place, or accolade. Others may be broader: concepts surrounding how you want your days to look, the type of legacy you want to leave, and the lifestyle that ignites your spirit. But right now, you're presented with an opportunity to go deeper. What is the *why* behind your goals? Where do your passions come from, and what is their origin story? How do your desires reflect deep, soulful needs? Are they linked to your childhood? Do they align with your past, or do they feel like brave declarations toward your future? In which ways do they illuminate your truth? Today, move beyond your list of aspirations and explore the root of their existence. Through this practice, you'll cultivate more powerful, sustainable, and purposeful intention—that's the frequency needed to craft successful manifestations.

How does love show up in your life?

You've got mail! And it's from, well, you! Today, you're invited to send yourself a letter as a form of manifestation. What are you looking to bring into your life? Perhaps it's romance, a new career path, clarity, or self-love. Whatever it is, write yourself a letter describing your intention, affirming that this magic is already on its way. Be your own cheerleader! Hype yourself up! Remind yourself why you deserve to receive exactly what you want—and don't hold back! Once you've written your letter, place it in an envelope, address it to yourself, put a stamp on it, and drop it in the mailbox. It will be delivered to you in a few days and, once it's received, you'll read it with a whole new perspective that is guaranteed to amplify your power.

The Knight of Swords is one of the most active cards in tarot. This dynamic scene features a young man in armor, riding a white horse at an incredible speed. Charging into battle, the knight raises his sword to the sky. His open mouth seems to call out a loud cry. This card is fierce, intense, and driven. When it appears, it signals a time when we are ready to take action on our ideas. There is a timely essence to the Knight of Swords, which means that we are—in fact—at the optimal moment for forward motion. Nothing can stop the Knight of Swords. Consider how you become moved and motivated by your own ideas. What is something you have been contemplating? Have you been hesitant to take the next step? If so, consider whether you're ready to launch into high gear. It may be time to ride.

262

When you give yourself permission to hold multiple truths simultaneously, you give yourself permission to be whole. To mirror the multitudes, complexities, and nuances intrinsic to your being. To honor the undulation of spirit and matter—the waxing and waning of light and shadow that moves across your sky of consciousness. To exist in flow, in thresholds, in space in-between. A powerful portal lives at the intersection of polarities. The key to unlocking this mystical pathway is your ability to embrace subtlety.

263

One of the easiest ways to ruin a manifestation is to fixate on it. When you become attached to an outcome, it will almost certainly become a bastardized version of what your heart hoped to receive. Right now, consider what hopes, wishes, or desires you can let go of. While it might seem like detaching from your manifestations decreases their power or stalls their progress, it is—in fact—the exact opposite. When we release, we allow the Universe to take the wheel. We trust the divine timing, the cosmic process, the mystical alchemy that connects the physical and astral planes, bringing magic into reality. So today, don't be afraid to let go, to release, to surrender.

Wearing a cape adorned with clouds mirroring the sky behind her, the Queen of Swords sits on a throne decorated with cherubs and butterflies. We see her in profile, with one hand pointing upward and the other holding a sword. She has a stern expression, as if she is in the process of making an important and serious decision. The Queen of Swords is a symbol of careful intellectual consideration. This card speaks to intention, deliberation, and decisiveness. After weighing the pros and cons, the Queen of Swords is ready to make a choice. There is an up-front and honest nature to this card. Right now, consider what that looks like for you. Have you processed, explored, contemplated all sides of the situation? Have you reviewed all the data and considered the best path forward? Today, think about how you can be direct, clear, and precise with your next steps.

Whatever you lost
was never truly yours.

266

Every day, we're inundated with so much information: influencers promoting products, tragedies reduced to memes, updates from distant relatives we haven't seen in decades. It's so much stimuli—presented so quickly!—how can we even begin to process and dissect the litany of content? And this happens every day, every hour, sometimes multiple times per hour, without considering its impact on our mind, body, or soul. Today, I invite you to reflect on your experience, how you feel, and what comes up for you emotionally as you scroll through your For You pages, timelines, and newsfeeds. Be gentle with yourself. Recognize the artificial stimulation that is undoubtedly penetrating every single aspect of your psyche. Consider how you can bring your awareness back to your body, your being, and to this moment in time: right now.

267

The full moon is the climax of the lunar cycle, and it occurs when the Moon and Sun are in direct opposition in the sky. As the Sun radiates on the celestial satellite, there is maximum illumination and the night sky is electrified by the Moon's vivid, silver glow. In the wild, nighttime predators are most active during this phase, which means our ancient ancestors were on the move, running, hiding, and preparing for invisible threats. They were on guard during the full moon, and even today, we may feel extra buzzy and alert during this phase. The full moon shines light on everything, so important discoveries are often made under this sky. We may choose to purge, release, or let things go during a full moon. No matter where you are in the current lunar cycle, consider how the energy of this phase—lucidity and implementation—shows up in your life.

268

They say not to go to sleep angry, as if conflict is the worst thing in the world. Sometimes we disagree with the people that we love, finding ourselves frustrated, disappointed, annoyed, triggered, bothered, or disturbed. Sometimes we need to heal—and recovery might not look like a quick apology. Reconciliation can't always happen between toothbrushing and face washings—it's not part of a bathroom routine. Just because you're upset doesn't mean everything's been ruined. Being angry is not a crime. Taking time and space to gain clarity is a blessing, and there's nothing wrong with needing to work through complicated emotions in your own unique way, on your own unique timeline. Don't deny your emotions. Give yourself permission to feel and to heal—give yourself permission to be truthful to your experience.

Break rules, push back, ask hard questions.

270

You're weird. And that's what I love about you. I only want to hang out with the weird ones—the ones who see the world through magical eyes. The ones who have a unique perspective on life, death, meaning, and magic. Why would you want to conform? Be the same as everyone else? It may be easier to blend in than stand out, but your soul chose your specific experience for a reason. Don't compromise your identity for the ease of homogeneity.

271

The King of Swords depicts His Majesty as he sits facing forward on a throne decorated with butterfly motifs. Wearing a long blue robe, he holds his sword up to the sky as clouds and birds drift in the wind behind him. This card symbolizes mental clarity, intellectual prowess, authority, confidence, and truth. It's the outcome of deep thoughts and rich, meaningful cognition, enabling us to understand all facets of a situation. The King of Swords remains cool, calm, and collected as the truth becomes clear. Right now, consider what you know to be real. What's something that you have meditated on and processed thoroughly, enabling you to have an easy confidence in your experience with it? What's something that you feel is resolved, or something that you've already solved in an honest and authentic way? These core intellectual values are an important part of your identity. So today, consider how you embody the King of Swords.

272

They say that everything is who you know. And that's absolutely true. We live in a social world. It's part of our human evolution. We live in a world that's supported and enhanced by our connections, communities, advocates, cheerleaders, family, friends, and peers. But not all of these connections need to be epic, cinematic ones. Not all of these connections need to look like a chance encounter with an important executive in an elevator who can sniff out your potential and change your life on the spot—or meeting the love of your life under an awning on a rainy day when you two decide to share an umbrella. While these types of over-the-top, grandiose bonds are beautiful, connections happen in powerful, subtle ways, too. Today, be mindful of the twinkles—of the encounters that you experience in the most ordinary places: an interaction with a cashier, making eye contact with a fellow dog walker, a familiar recognition of someone on the bus. This is the essence of magic within the mundane.

Since time immemorial, fire has been revered for its ferocious transformational power. It can create (think: heat, food sanitization, community gatherings), and it can destroy (think: wildfires, arson, third-degree burns). Moreover, it's believed that flame creates a bridge between the physical and spiritual realms. Candles encapsulate this power. When you light a candle, you amplify your intentions and engage transformational forces. Ever notice how a few candles can shift the energy of an environment? That's a simple form of candle magic. In modern magical practice, candles can be used to amplify any kind of manifestation—for both letting go or bringing in. One of the simplest rituals you can perform involves lighting a candle, saying your intention into the flame, and extinguishing the flame to release your intention into the Universe. Magic doesn't need to be complex; your energy is what ignites meaning into the ritual.

Believe in yourself.
The rest will follow.

The Ace of Cups is the first card in the Cups suit. This card depicts a mysterious hand emerging from a cloud, holding a golden chalice. Four streams of water pour from the cup—into a lotus-filled pond below—while a dove nosedives into the vessel. The Cups suit in tarot speaks to emotions, intuition, imagination, feelings, and internal truths. Cups are both what we offer to others in the form of spiritual truth, as well as what is inside the cup—the contents, the depth, the meaning. The Ace of Cups symbolizes raw, untethered, spiritual energy. It represents feelings, intentions, and divine guidance. The gentle honesty of this card and its representation of pure feelings and sensations is empowering. Right now, consider how you can connect with your emotional truths. What do they feel like, look like, and embody for you? Scan your heart. What is your intuition communicating? There's no need to over-intellectualize with the Ace of Cups. This energy is straight from the soul.

Inspiration is everywhere. It's baked into the things that you love as well as the things that you hate. Inspiration is infused into the liminal, the gray areas, and the spaces that feel both empty and overly occupied. It's in nature and in cities. It's in movement and stillness. It's in words, actions, thoughts, meanings. What's inspiring you right now? Without overthinking, notice the first thing that pops into your mind and give yourself permission to explore that train of thought, flow of creativity, and thread of meaning.

You're invited to tap into your own personal power by diving deep beneath the surface. It takes courage to look at our own thorny innards, but acknowledging your self-doubts, anxieties, and questionable behaviors (both from the past and in the present) is a necessary step in fortifying personal agency. Today, ask yourself the following questions: What secrets are you keeping from others? What are you hiding from yourself? How can you honor both your vulnerability and bravery, recognizing that these are ultimately one and the same? How do you plunge into the darkness, while still honoring and respecting your light?

In the Two of Cups, we see a couple linked through alchemy, magic, and spiritual connection. The roles are reversed, with the female figure wearing the crown of laurels and the male figure wearing the rose circlet. This symbolizes a deep and powerful emotional exchange—two people who are willing to trade experiences, share narratives, and understand each other empirically and empathetically. With the Two of Cups, there is a sense of safety, respect, and commitment. The figures in these cards are symbolizing the power of true, emotional alliance. Right now, think about what soulful relationships you have in your life. Is it with a lover or a friend? Perhaps a mentor or a family member? Who do you trust to hold space for your vast and complex emotional truths? And what does it look like when you support their journey in return? Find gratitude for those individuals in your life, recognizing that you don't need an entire army of people to support you. Just a few close confidants are really all it takes.

Destiny is a river.
Go with the flow.

Perhaps you are—right now—at a turning point in your narrative. Is it time to make a change? Take a step? Move in a different direction? You may not have all the information just yet, so don't be afraid to rely on external resources to illuminate the road in front of you, especially guidance from close companions. Friends, family, colleagues, and trusted guides can light your way. Remember, your decisions belong to you, but the journey doesn't have to be a solitary one. Maybe, this time, you don't have to walk alone.

During the waning gibbous phase, a distinctive shadow slowly crawls across the Moon's face, growing wider, darker, and richer with each passing moment. In the aftermath of the electric full moon, when new information is revealed, the waning gibbous begins to process the wisdom, carefully separating and distinguishing fact from fiction. When the Moon is in its waning gibbous phase, we're compelled to disseminate information, share our learnings, and work with others in community to connect the dots. No matter where you are in the current lunar cycle, consider how the energy of this phase—discernment and communication—shows up in your life.

Several years ago, when trying to explain the extraordinary synchronicities, patterns, and repetitions that define this magical life, I stated "there are no coincidences," which became an acronym (TANC), which became an expression. Used similarly to how *jinx* is exclaimed when two people accidentally say the same word or phrase in union, TANC calls out those magical moments of connectivity. But TANC is more than just a phrase—it's a lifestyle. Right now, open your senses to the intricate dance of cosmic synchronicity that weaves patterns of meaning throughout your journey. Like constellations forming stories, moments of alignment carry messages from the Universe. Reflect on times in your life when seemingly unrelated events converged to form a coherent narrative—these threads of synchronicity serve as a reminder that there's a hidden harmony in the chaos, a universal rhythm guiding your steps. These TANCs happen for a reason; they're breadcrumbs leading you toward your true self, affirming your soul's unique vibration. And, naturally, you're receiving this message at exactly the right moment. That's what we call TANC.

We represent different things to different people, and we carry these multitudes—others' perspectives of us—within our psyche. Find peace with these various versions of you, recognizing that these multicolored hues aren't conflicts, they're enhancements. You are prismatic.

284

Your inner knowing is a direct line to the Divine—a sacred channel through which messages and guidance flow without judgment or limitation. And yes, sometimes, you receive feedback that may not immediately make sense, but by cultivating a safe and protected relationship with your inner knowing, you'll move beyond the urge to control, prescribe, and classify. Wondering how to strengthen your intuition? Gently close or lower your eyes, and ask your higher self for a shape, image, word, or color to illuminate this moment. Don't overthink it; just let something pop into your mind's eye. Do you have it? Great—what is it? Ask your higher self why that symbol arrived in your psyche. What does it want you to know? What is it trying to communicate? Why did your higher self express itself in that form? Again, no judgments and no overthinking. This is an exchange between soul and ego. By strengthening your intuitive abilities and nurturing your connection to deep wisdom, you'll be guided in unexpected ways that transcend the ordinary. Follow that path.

The Three of Cups is truly a vibe. In this card, three figures are depicted, all holding chalices to the sky and dancing around an abundant harvest. These three individuals radiate a spirit of joy, celebration, creativity, and community—true happiness exudes from this iconography. Each individual is recognized, appreciated, and celebrated. This card emphasizes the importance of play. It reminds us that emotional experiences should includes fun, merriment, and revelry. In fact, in order for us to experience complete spiritual landscapes, we need to *enjoy* the process of being alive. Today, consider whether you've been allocating enough time for joy. If not, this is an excellent moment to make plans with people who share your lust for life, your hobbies, your interests—people you know you can always have a good time with. Remember, pleasure is a spiritual practice.

286

Things might not make sense right now. Things may feel unfair, unkind, cruel, too slow, too fast, or simply out of step. But one day, all this timing, all of your patience, and all of your frustrations—the limited perspective you have right now—will make sense. One day you'll look back on these unknowns with gratitude. You'll appreciate the way these stories unfolded and how the narratives appeared in your life exactly when you were ready to receive them. You'll know that the divine timing has always been working in your favor. So today, remember that the things that don't make sense right now will surely be clarified.

287

Mundane magic is a practice that infuses your everyday tasks and habits with intention and mysticism. Today, explore an intention you'd like to foster. Is it confidence? Courage? Connection? Once you've tuned in to its energy, perform your morning routine. For example, perhaps your intention is determination. Depending on your routine, you may wash your face, imagining the water washing away self-doubt and stagnancy. You may choose to wear brightly hued lipstick for an energy boost or clothing that makes you feel empowered, emboldened, and creative. Don't overthink this process! There's no right or wrong way to do this—fundamentally, you're forming a deeper alignment with your soul's truth. You can't get it wrong.

What's one brave thing
you can do today?

Sometimes, messages from the other side can be strong, clear, and direct—we know exactly who's contacting us and what they're saying, and perhaps we can even dialogue with them through metaphysical channels. Other times, connections are expressed through subtle, sensory experiences: scents, breezes, light shining into your bedroom. Whether we refer to these otherworldly entities as ghosts, spirits, ancestors, angels, guides, or something else, today you're invited to explore the concept of supernatural suspension, moving fluidly between dimensions by treating every notable twinkle or intrigue as a welcome salutation.

You're not responsible for others' emotions. You're not responsible for others' wounds. You're not responsible for others' healing. Or feelings. Or what people do with their pain. Sensitive folk like us feel an innate sense of duty—that unique blend of compassion and trauma, likely absorbed before you were old enough to understand its implications. But today, you are wise enough to know that while you can guide a horse to water, you cannot make them drink. You can apologize. You can empathize. You can even problem-solve. But, when all is said and done, you cannot change others' past, present, or future. You cannot undo their hurt, and you cannot right their wrong. Support the people you love. Encourage them. Cheer them on. And trust that they, just like you, are entitled to their own experiences.

Did you know that your passions, interests, hobbies, and proclivities are all expressions of your soul? All the things that intrigue you—music, art, jokes, design, writing, magic—call out to you for a reason. Your passions aren't arbitrary, they're messages. Today, pick one thing you enjoy and consider why you like it. What feelings does it evoke? What does it remind you of? What does it conjure within your being? And, perhaps most importantly, if you were to explore it from a bird's-eye view, what does it say about you? Pleasures are imprints of your spirit's presence. Don't overlook their magic.

The Four of Cups depicts an individual sitting beneath a tree—legs crossed and arms folded—as an unexpected miracle appears to his right. Somehow, from out of nowhere, a hand carrying a chalice emerges from a puff of smoke. This is nothing short of divine! But our central character is fixated on the three empty cups in front of them, unaware of the extraordinary magic right under their nose. This card symbolizes a fixation on what we do not have, what we have lost, what we're disappointed by—and all the ways these letdowns are preventing us from seeing new opportunities ahead. This card reminds us that we are presented with offerings, magic, and miracles all the time, but it's our sole responsibility to pay attention to the Universe's blessings. Right now, reflect on whether you have been fixated on what you are lacking. Could that be skewing your perspective to the extent that you're overlooking the amazing fortunes just beginning to unfold?

Creativity is a sponge: sometimes you're absorbing, sometimes you're releasing. Which phase are you in right now?

294

Today, consider exploring what comes naturally to you—as well as where you need to put in more work, time, and elbow grease. Just observe and consider the different ways your body, soul, and mind experience a variety of input and output. Are you someone who wakes up first thing in the morning and gets straight into your day? Or are you someone who needs a slow and easy routine to get acclimated? Are you someone who dives headfirst into new projects and ideas? Or is the idea of beginning something from scratch daunting—would you rather research, plan, and strategize before making a major move? Simply observe where your energy falls organically, recognizing how your individual qualities are a beautiful testament to your soul's own sacred experience.

295

At the last quarter moon (also known as the third quarter moon), we've returned to 50 percent illumination. The shadow has flipped 180 degrees from its position during the first quarter moon, which means new information is being revealed, while other wisdoms are being concealed. At this time, we have the ability to determine whether we've been productive, successful, and fruitful in realizing our intentions. This phase presents an opportunity to review what's worked and what hasn't worked, and make any final adjustments. No matter where you are in the current lunar cycle, consider how the energy of this phase—assessment and analysis—shows up in your life.

296

Are you trying to re-create an experience, a feeling, a relationship, or a dynamic that happened in the past? Are you seeking that same type of love? That same kind of validation? That same moment of connection? If so, you're focusing on the impossible. Every single moment, experience, and encounter is different. You can never re-create what happened in the past. But that isn't a bad thing—every moment is filled with its own irreproducible alchemical potential. You can spiritually optimize for the things that have brought you pleasure, prioritizing the sensations that electrified your being. But you're not limited to the experiences that you've already had. Your life can—and will—surpass even the happiest times and the most precious memories. Don't give up on your future.

You're not going to want to hear this, but not every opportunity needs to be yours. Not every raise or promotion or moment in the spotlight is for you. We are all on our own timelines and trajectories, taking turns. Waxing and waning in our efforts. Oscillating through periods of abundance and reorganization. Although it may be frustrating to see others celebrating their achievements, trust that your own timeline will appropriately reflect your journey. Rather than compare yourself to someone else's timeline, trust that you are on the path that's best suited for you. You will have all the moments you need.

You are your own responsibility.
Let this empower you.
Let this embolden you.
Let this set you free.

The Five of Cups is a scene of mourning. The central figure wears a long, black cape with their head positioned downward, back facing us. We see three cups knocked over with their contents spilled on the floor. The tone is sorrowful and ominous, and there's certainly an atmosphere of loss. Accordingly, this card represents a period of grief, mourning, or sadness. Damage has been done, and we must take time to reflect. However, behind the central figure, two cups remain upright, symbolizing an important qualification. All hope is not lost. Similarly, this card reminds us that it is more than okay to take time to grieve. Embracing your sadness is a necessary part of this moment, but don't lose yourself to the enormity of these feelings. There is hope. There is potential. There are components to the circumstances that have not yet been explored. This intensity is not permanent, and you will persevere, coming out stronger on the other side.

300

Some days, the best that you can do is almost nothing at all. Some days, you're going to feel unproductive, unmotivated, exhausted, and uninspired. You're going to feel like your efforts are not worth it, and that you can't take on the extra task, let alone tackle your to-do list. Some days, you won't be able to motivate yourself or push forward. And that's okay. In fact, these days are an important part of our human experience. They're humbling, reflective. In their own strange way, they're nourishing and supportive—they provide us with insight into our limits and boundaries. Give these days permission to exist without judgment or criticism. Trust that these days are valid, meaningful, and beautiful, too.

When in doubt,
find the simplest solution.

Freezer magic is a powerful tool mystics employ to rid themselves of burdens and toxic energy. Today, you're invited to perform a freezer ritual. Grab a journal, paper, pen, and string. Find a quiet place in your house where you can settle and perform this ritual undisturbed. For several minutes, journal about any dynamics you'd like to "freeze," or remove, from your life. After you've journaled, identify the major energy, people, situations, and/or circumstances you'd like to put on ice. Write these on a piece of paper, then bind it, wrapping it in string. Once you're done, place it in your freezer. So mote it be.

The Tower card is dramatic, to say the least. This card depicts a vertical structure—the presumed tower—struck by lightning, with figures falling to their deaths from the burning windows. While this imagery is disturbing, it overflows with metaphor and symbolism. When we look at the tower, we see that it was built on the very top of a mountain peak—a precarious place to construct a giant vertical tower! The poor planning of this structure is an important detail: it reveals that whatever is falling apart—for you, on a personal level—was never truly built to last. It didn't have the scalability or sustainability, and there was no way it could possibly withstand any dramatic climactic event. It was only a matter of time before the structure collapsed. The Tower card represents major changes in your life—shifts that completely alter how you decide to move forward. Right now, consider if there are any major pivots taking place in your life, and whether they're disrupting systems that weren't sound in the first place. The Tower card doesn't suggest that something solid is doomed for destruction, but rather points to whatever circumstances in your life were precarious and unreliable from the start.

Exhaustion isn't necessarily a bad sign. Exhaustion could mean that you're going through a tremendous transformational growth spurt. Your psyche may be desperately seeking rest because it is expanding and transforming at such extraordinary rates that only sleep can help regulate this profound metamorphosis. Exhaustion could mean that you're blossoming at unprecedented speeds. Exhaustion could mean that you're on the precipice of a tremendous awakening. So right now, if you feel exhausted, consider the possibility that it may indicate a dynamic growth spurt. Let yourself be tired.

What are the clouds
telling you today?

The sweet scene in the Six of Cups depicts youthful innocence. In this card, the six cups are filled with daffodils, a symbol of spring, youth, and new beginnings. Two small children stand facing each other, with one offering the other this gentle bouquet. The relationship here is pure, innocent, playful, and childlike. The card invites us to consider the softer side of our emotions. It asks us to think back to some happy, nostalgic memories and recall times before life became overcomplicated. What was the emotional experience of falling in love for the first time? What does it feel like for you to return to some of the soft, gentle, romantic moments from your past? Preserving these tender sentiments is an important part of our holistic healing journey—occasionally basking in nostalgia is good for the soul.

Speculation is the enemy of communication.

308

If you've reached the point where absolutely everything someone does annoys you, take space. Create distance. Set a boundary. You've entered a phase of reactivity that is no longer rooted in reality but rather steeped in deep wounds pouring over like volcanoes. Give yourself time to breathe before continuing forward; the cells need to be reoxygenated before you can see clearly again.

The lunar cycle concludes with the waning crescent phase, a splinter of light on a darkening Moon. As the Moon prepares to close out its cycle, there is nothing left to do but reflect; by this point, all the work has been done. We've moved through intentions, implementations, and disseminations; what once existed no longer functions in its original form. It has been forever changed. And we, too, have been forever changed. Under this dark sky, we're inspired to reflect on growth. This is an excellent time to process, ruminate, and practice self-care. No matter where you are in the current lunar cycle, consider how the energy of this phase—completion and departure—shows up in your life.

What is your relationship to your dreams? Are your dreams long, surreal, unusual, and fantastical, or are they re-creations of your day-to-day life? Are they short, realistic, and empowering, or are they anxiety-inducing? Do you experience premonitions, or do your dreams feel like a true unfolding of all of the stimuli you experience in your conscious life? Today, simply observe your relationship to your dreamscape without judgment. Consider how your dreams might offer insight into the vast abyss that is your subconscious. What would it feel like to go even further into your psyche? When you go to sleep tonight, invite your psyche to reveal even more wisdom, insight, and clarity. Ask your subconscious to take you somewhere and offer you an adventure that wouldn't be possible in the physical realm. Give your dreams permission to be wild and see how they respond to that instruction.

Be kind to your mind.

312

You might encounter false starts or empty promises, or get really close to that feeling of achievement, only for it to fall flat and spiral into yet another letdown. This doesn't mean that you're fated to live a bleak existence. In fact, it reflects the extraordinary magnitude of your unique journey—that your path is wider, richer, and deeper than most circumstances could contain. You won't be in alignment with your soul's mission every single day, but over the course of your lifetime, you'll be continuously rerouted back on your path. If you find yourself frustrated by the process, find appreciation for the fact that your journey is truly divinely led. And that is a special type of existence.

313

The Star card in tarot is about stripping down to the basics. It's about connecting with your hopes, wishes, dreams, and ideas, and finding new ways to channel your personal aspirations into collective healing. The Star card depicts a nude figure with two water vessels that are being poured out. Water, a symbol of intuition, nourishment, and life, is flowing abundantly, while stars twinkle overhead. Fundamentally, the Star card supports our connection to greater pursuits—to healing, faith, and humanity. It's a reminder that your magic is amplified when you tap into the collective. When you consider not just what benefits you individually, but *also* the greater good, extraordinary things can happen.

314

Stop going through life expecting people to read your mind, or expecting that the timing needs to follow a particular timeline. Stop going through life feeling disappointed that people, situations, or opportunities didn't present themselves in the rigid, constructed narrative that you created, based on jealousy, competition, fear, lack, and scarcity. Instead, *start* living authentically. *Start* trusting the timing of the Universe. *Start* recognizing the blessings and bounty you experience every single day—the beautiful twists and turns that define existence. Start appreciating the magic of every single moment.

You can drastically improve your relationships by listening. At the end of the day, most people just want to be heard, to feel validated, to be appreciated. In conversation, acknowledge what is being said. Tune in to words, mannerisms, and energetic expressions. Resist the urge to be defensive, to redirect focus back to yourself, or to trivialize others' problems. Focus on absorbing as much information as you can and asking thoughtful questions that add various dimensions to the dialogue. And sometimes, being quiet is best. Sometimes it's best to just let words be messy and meander in circles, or have no clear direction at all. Sometimes, just witnessing another's experience is all anyone really needs.

Nothing changes
if nothing changes.

In the Seven of Cups, we see a shadowy figure whose back is facing us as they contemplate the seven cups emerging from a cloud in front of them. Each of these cups has a different offering: jewels and gems, snakes and demonic entities. There's a laurel wreath that looks inviting, but it's perched on a cup that has a skull etched into its facade—certainly a risky sign. There's even a mystery cup: the object is covered by a piece of fabric and emanates an eerie red aura. What will it be? With the Seven of Cups, we are enticed by the potential of each opportunity. But is it real or an illusion? Consider how the Seven of Cups is showing up in your own life. Are you finding yourself seduced by possibility? Be careful, because things may not be as they seem. When we move impulsively or from a place of ego, it prevents us from being able to use sound judgment to explore the authentic experiences ahead. Fantasy is not real life, and the Seven of Cups reminds us how important it is to stay grounded in truth.

Take up space.

Today, take a break from manifesting. Take a break from wanting, desiring, anticipating, from planting seeds, setting intentions, and demanding more. Today, simply focus on what you have. Take inventory of what already exists. Observe the blessings in your life—both large and small. Shift your narrative from demanding to surrendering. Inhale the bounty that is your life. Find gratitude. Find motion. Find gentle calm. After all, how will you know your desires are still relevant if you don't take a moment to catch your breath?

320

The Eight of Cups depicts a mysterious twilight scene in the foreground. Eight cups are stacked on each other, and our central character is pictured walking away. The only witness, the eclipsed full moon, watches knowingly as this person flees the scene. Indeed, this card represents an intentional exit, perhaps leaving before the task has been completed. We're abandoning. We're withdrawing. Maybe we're even escaping. And, in the Eight of Cups, the central character is getting away with it, too. It seems that they will be able to leave unnoticed—and hopefully unscathed. This card reminds us that sometimes we need to walk away. Sure, we may have invested time, energy, and resources into an endeavor, but if we intuitively know that it is not supporting our best interests, we may need to change course to quit while we're ahead. At what point in your life have you made the difficult decision to walk away? And how did that choice empower you? One of the most amazing parts of being human is our ability to change our mind. Never forget that you have agency in every action and reaction.

Your reality mirrors your psyche.
Your psyche mirrors your reality.

Like the celestial bodies, we're constantly moving through seasons with a deeper understanding of self and others. There's change and flow; things go up and down. We are healing. And even when healing doesn't feel like healing, we are. Trust your orbit.

Today, give yourself permission to loosen your tight grip on control. Experiment. Explore. Escape. Meander through the corners of your mind, put pen to paper (or brush to canvas) and see what emerges. Allow yourself to journey through different forms of consciousness, steep yourself in wonder, and invite your inner child to express themself. While imagination and creativity are often deemed superfluous or indulgent against the backdrop of capitalism, they're essential components of self-actualization and collective freedom. If we can't imagine different, better, richer, brighter possibilities, how will we enact change?

324

There's an adage that I contemplate often: "You are the average of the five people you spend the most time with." This concept suggests that the closest individuals in our lives profoundly influence our thoughts, passions, and even our behaviors. No matter how unique we think we are, we're biologically susceptible to external influences. We radiate what we receive. Today, consider how your community shapes your perception of the world. What subjects dominate your conversations? What shared interests do you have? What are your collective ethics, ideologies, and philosophies? And where do you see room for improvement? For example, when I first began confronting my eating disorders and body dysmorphia, I realized my friends were in active addiction. The constant exposure to toxic rhetoric surrounding bodies and beauty was deeply impacting my psyche and hindering my healing. With my therapist, we agreed that I needed boundaries. We can't change others, but we have the power to craft our reality. We can create guidelines and establish expectations for our interactions. We can monitor what we absorb. Right now, I encourage you to heighten your awareness of the reflections you radiate, ensuring that they're aligned with your truth.

Everyone talks about the importance of gratitude. In fact, the term has become so popular, so mainstream, it can start to feel inauthentic and hackneyed. Like factory-produced wall art dictating *good vibes only,* or wine glasses that tell us—in glittering cursive—*to live laugh love.* And while this hyper-commodification can sometimes reflect the superficiality of a concept, in the case of gratitude, it's merely the simplified mass adoption of a significant spiritual practice. Because gratitude is genuinely powerful. By establishing a gratitude practice, the Universe knows what you want, what you appreciate, and it rewards you accordingly. Alternatively, when we focus on lack, scarcity, or voids, the Universe believes *this* is our preferred energetic focus. Yes, the Universe starts to believe that you *enjoy* being stressed. At best, it maintains your tension; at worst, it multiplies the deficit. Right now, reflect on your gratitude. Speak it out loud ("I am grateful for . . .") and let the warm feeling of appreciation radiate through your psychic and physical body like a cup of hot cocoa on a cold winter night. Embrace your abundance, and let that attract more, more, more. So mote it be.

326

When you find yourself wading in the murky water, remember the vast, boundless oceans that exist beyond the horizon. In these aquatic expanses, everything is part of a whole. Our feelings. Our experiences. Our memories. They're all microcosms in the greater macrocosm. So don't be afraid of your prickly sensitivities as clay swirls around your feet on the shore. Let your emotions move through you like a crystal stream—let them empower you like hydraulics. Remember that the delicate details of your psyche will always mirror the collective. Your feelings are valid.

"*Want to see something cool?*" That's the essence of the Nine of Cups. In this card, a central figure sits on a bench, surrounded and framed by nine glistening golden cups positioned on a display table, elegantly draped with a blue tablecloth. The individual sits with their arms crossed, a smile on their face, and a genuine expression of pride and satisfaction. They are proud of their accomplishments and aren't afraid to tell you about them. There is a sense of fulfillment and completion, and perhaps a *tinge* of arrogance—but, ultimately, their infectious jolliness exudes genuine pride. What are you proud of? What brings you a sense of fulfillment? What are you eager to showcase and present? How do you talk about your accomplishments? Today, remember that there's nothing wrong with exploring —and sharing—your satisfaction. The people who love you and support you are delighted to hear about the things that bring you pleasure! Relishing in your achievements is an important part of your spiritual happiness. So while you obviously don't want to come off as cocky or entitled, right now, remember that it's important and meaningful to celebrate your wins.

I'm a slow writer. It takes me time to weave my words on a page. I appreciate my meticulous detail, but my scrutiny does, sometimes, get in the way of what I am trying to say. The best writing advice I've ever heard—and that I actively attempt to implement—is *just write*. Put words on the page. Keep going. Don't worry about perfection or poetry or sentence structure. Just get your ideas down. Bring ideas to life. In a way, this is a beautiful metaphor for what it means to live, be present and exist purely in the moment. Of course, it's not going to be perfect. Of course, it's not going to be refined. Of course, it's not always going to make sense. But just as we must write, we must live. We must keep going. It's a testament to the beautiful relationship and interconnectivity between creativity and existence.

What a gift it is to feel so incredibly deeply.

330

Ego, in and of itself, isn't necessarily bad. Ego helps us establish standards, maintain confidence, and acknowledge worth. It helps us show up, take up space, and have the courage to overcome life's chronic obstacles. We want to be our own strong, fierce cheerleaders, hyping ourselves up again and again and again. In that context, ego is an asset. But we all know what can happen when ego gets out of control—it can ruin *everything*, preventing us from seeing clearly. Tempting us with deceit. But, then again, too little ego is escape, delusion, martyrdom. It's easy to dissolve when you have nothing holding you together in the first place. Indeed, having *no ego* can be just as problematic as having *too much ego*. Today, consider how you facilitate your own checks-and-balances system: How can you embrace passionate movement, while still maintaining a soulful, mystical connection? What does it look like to have *just enough* ego to get something started, paired with *just enough* humility to maintain perspective? What does it look like to flow between everything and nothing? Remember, these dimensions aren't at odds—they're in harmony.

331

The Moon is an incredibly powerful celestial body. A bright, beautiful, oversized Moon always commands attention. We stop and stare. Whether we like it or not, we feel the magnetic vibration of this celestial satellite. Likewise, the Moon card in tarot depicts a similar scene, as all creatures—from land and sea—emerge to experience the Moon's profound magnetism. In this card, we see both a domestic and a feral dog howling wildly into the night sky, symbolizing how powerful emotions can be. We may feel that we're contained, responsible, sophisticated, and mature, but the Moon—a symbol of our own internal worlds and intuition—is more powerful than our ability to be buttoned up and refined. The Moon makes us wild. And so can our emotions. Often, in these untamed expressions of psyche, the best thing we can do is recognize how powerless we are when it comes to our raw, uninhibited psyche. Right now, consider how your emotions—untamed, unabashed, feral—impact your reality when you surrender to the instinctual parts of your being.

As Sagittarian author Joan Didion perfectly articulated, "We tell ourselves stories in order to live." Indeed, perhaps the most distinctly human thing about being, well, distinctly human is the ability to fictionalize. To fantasize. To dream. Perhaps life doesn't always need to be rational. Perhaps life is meant to be romantic. Perhaps we can give ourselves permission to tap into our infinite well of creativity—creating wider, richer, more textural narratives, and decorating the mundane with allegory, symbolism, and meaning. Maybe existing doesn't need to be so literal. Maybe it's metaphoric, or poetic, or literary. The meaning of life could be to reinvent its meaning every single day. So, my beautiful friend, what's your purpose today? I encourage you to make it a juicy one. After all, this is your odyssey. You write the story.

You're not your thoughts,
and you're not your feelings.
They're visitors, just
passing through.

The Ten of Cups is a true revelatory scene. We see a couple, standing close, with their arms outstretched to the sky, taking in all the goodness overhead—a beautiful arched rainbow with 10 golden cups embedded in the prism—while two children frolic at their side. This scene is a depiction of joy, happiness, and future achievements, all by way of trusting one's intuition. The display of cups reflects the bounty that comes from honest spiritual development. In this card, we see an idyllic family scene with a beautiful connection to the Divine. Today, trust that when you give yourself permission to embrace your emotions, mystical truths, deep wisdom, and powerful intuition—fully and completely—you're moving toward your highest and best self. Fortune favors those who live bravely and authentically. By embracing the exquisite complexities of your soul, you set yourself up for a magnificent life ahead.

Sometimes loneliness just needs you to acknowledge its existence.

336

You're allowed to feel good. To feel the corners of your lips curl upward, stretching your cheeks in a wide smile. You're allowed to laugh, letting tears build up in your eyes as you exhale mighty, rhythmic, rumbling howls—fearless and unfettered. You're allowed to have dessert, to experience the rich cacophony of decadent flavors sinking into your tongue. You're allowed to take up space and live boldly. You're allowed to be endlessly wild, like the dissonant yelps of coyotes across twilight's expansive horizon. Right now, give yourself permission to tap into those limitless expanses of joy, pleasure, and delight. Remember what it feels like to be alive.

337

Your memories are threads that weave the tapestry of your beautiful, complex, expansive life. By revisiting these encounters with gentle curiosity, you may uncover patterns, themes, and spiritual wisdom, exposing new pathways for transformation. Today, give yourself permission to surrender to nostalgia. What's calling out to you right now, and how does that relate to your current conditions? How do these memories impact your life today?

So what if everyone else is sprinting? How does their speed serve you? You're not on their timeline. You're not on their path. You're not in their race. After all, you glide. You float. You transcend. You simply arrive.

339

Are you waiting until you're more settled to begin something? Are you waiting until you have found perfection in one area or multiple areas of life before you take the risk, diving headfirst into a new endeavor? Are you waiting for a green light? For permission? Or for someone or something to tell you that you're ready? If so, consider this your invitation. You don't need to wait anymore. Nothing is ever perfect. That's the whole point. You don't need everything to be symmetrically aligned before taking the next step and moving toward your hopes, dreams, and wishes. Whether it is looking for love, starting a new endeavor, or giving yourself the opportunity to begin again, this right now is your confirmation that you are ready. That you shouldn't wait another month or week or day—because that refined experience you were chasing is an impossible projection. It's fear manifesting itself through perfectionism. So today, let go of it and just get started. You'll thank yourself tomorrow.

340

Energy goes where intention flows. Today, consider where you've been focusing your attention. Are you fixating on all of the things you don't have yet—on all of the disappointments, rejections, and feelings of inadequacy? Or are you directing your gaze toward the potential, the possibilities, the exciting expressions that have yet to be revealed? Whatever you are focusing on will be amplified. So right now, consider where you're placing your awareness, and be specific about where you want to redirect that divine energy.

341

You don't need to ascend to the 5D (or whatever the current terminology is) to access your intuitive, psychic abilities. In fact, connecting with those innate skills is an extremely grounded, rooted, and terrestrial experience. The more anchored you are, the easier it will be to access your sharp extrasensory perceptions. When we step away from the mental noise—that incessant, cerebral clambering—we're invited into our psychic powers as we become more connected to our raw, mammalian nature. Our extrasensory abilities are part of what makes us human; they're baked into our DNA. Just as other animals use their myriad senses to detect dangers, we humans use a host of skills to understand both explicit and implicit situations. Our external senses—sight, sound, smell, taste, and touch—help us understand the tangible world, but our intuitive senses connect us to the truths that exist beyond the physical sector. Beyond the veil. Today, consider how you receive psychic information. Is it through your thoughts? Your feelings? Your vision? We all have different skills that manifest in different ways. Everyone metabolizes extrasensory connections in their own unique way; as always, there's no right or wrong. It's simply about learning how to work with your own intuitive sensibilities. Learning how to become—and surrender—to your innate humanness.

It's painful to step away from potential. But potential isn't real. Potential isn't commitment. I know potential might feel genuine. It might feel like the closest you've ever gotten to what you truly desire— like it was right there. Like you could almost taste it. And perhaps you think: if only it had matured *just* a bit longer, it would've been perfect. But that's exactly what distinguishes potential from authenticity. Potential is a concept, a veneer, a mirror that reflects what you genuinely crave. Potential is a guide, not an absolute, so don't be afraid to distance yourself from the facade. Trust the real thing is coming, and when it does, you'll surely know the difference.

Transform until your soul is free.

Just as a mirror reflects your external visage, so too can it reveal the depths of your soul and the essence of your being. Find a quiet space and sit before your reflection. Gaze into your own eyes, those windows to your inner world. In this connection, witness the journey you've embarked upon, the triumphs and tribulations that have shaped your path. Soften any self-judgment or doubt and find yourself—you, who has always been with yourself—affirming your existence. As you peer into your reflection, speak kind words, acknowledging your strengths and honoring the lessons you've learned. Let these statements reverberate through your being, anchoring you with appreciation and gratitude. Now, with courage, explore the layers beneath the surface. What dreams lie dormant? What aspirations whisper in the corners of your heart? Acknowledge any fears or doubts that arise, for they, too, are part of your authentic tapestry. In this sacred encounter with your own reflection, you forge a profound connection with your true self. As you honor your essence, you invite a harmonious alignment with your inner desires and external manifestations. Remember, as you embrace your authentic reflection, you gracefully embrace power, radiance, and truth.

In the Page of Cups, we see a central figure wearing a blue beret and a tunic decorated with lotus flowers, accented by a long, flowing scarf, which gives the figure an almost aquatic essence. He stands on a shore, and a river flows behind him. In his hand, he holds a gold cup filled with water, from which a small, blue fish emerges. He smiles at the fish, both knowingly and in amusement. Likewise, this card symbolizes the surprising, yet familiar, emergence of our own intuition. The Page of Cups represents those unexpected psychic pings, knee-jerk sensitivities, and gut feelings. There's an innocence present as well, illuminating the gentle nature of cultivating a relationship with our psychic world. Today, consider how you feel when you receive those dreamy, unexpected messages from your subconscious. How do you greet them? How do you honor them? What does it feel like to incorporate that mystical magic into your life?

346

Did you know that while *flora* refers to the plant life of an area, *fauna* refers not just to animals, but also to spirit life? Today, you're invited to explore your profound connection with the primal energies of the natural world—to tune in to the whispers of the creatures and enchanted entities that share our planet. Perhaps you're being guided to observe the behaviors and characteristics of specific animals that appear in your surroundings or dreams. Or maybe you're exploring the intangible, electric energy that emanates from a forest, meadow, park, or tree. Know that you don't just possess an innate connection to the natural world and its rhythms—you *are* that flow. Never forget that you're nature, baby. Both flora and fauna. Don't be afraid to get wild.

You're messy and imperfect.

And you're worthy of endless, boundless, love— exactly as you are.

In tarot, the Sun card depicts a small child riding on a white horse—perhaps the same horse depicted in the Death card—waving a long, velvety red flag parading across a field of sunflowers. Against the backdrop of an enormous glowing sun, this is victory. This is happiness. This is true, unabashed bliss. The Sun card is a powerful testament to joy, childhood excitement, pleasure, and the rare moments when everything goes *right*. What does it mean to feel truly and completely satisfied? What does it feel like when you get everything that you want? To bask in the incredible bliss of your hopes and desires *actually* coming to fruition? The Sun card reminds us that we need to make room for the possibility that everything goes according to plan. And when it does, we need to celebrate and honor the incredible fortune of things working out in our favor. The Sun card reminds us that part of this journey is accepting that life can—in fact—be spectacular. Right now, imagine yourself receiving all the things that you hope to receive, and achieving all the things you hope to achieve. Can you give yourself permission to enjoy them without stipulations? The Sun card invites you to experiment with that sensation.

Rejection is protection.

And rejection is redirection.

Be wary of trying to meet others' expectations. Their projections have nothing to do with your reality. So when you feel that icy shiver of external judgment creeping up your spine, shake wildly like a wet dog. The only person you have to impress is yourself.

In the Knight of Cups, we see a knight riding on a white horse while holding a golden cup in his hand. He's dressed in armor, his tunic decorated with fish, symbolizing a connection to the psychic world. The wings on his helmet and shoes are an allusion to Mercury, the god of communication. The horse is in motion, albeit moving calmly and carefully. There's a slow and graceful nature to this scene, exuding ease and intentionality. What does it feel like when we trust ourselves enough to move at a pace that is divinely guided, that is thoughtful and intentional? A pace that doesn't force or rush? Right now, consider how you can listen to your heart, your truth, and your intuition without making any impulsive, sudden movements. How can you navigate forward, while also maintaining a careful rhythm that protects your gentle sensitivities? Fundamentally, this card is about preserving your energy so you don't burn out. Think about what that means for you today.

352

You cannot exist exclusively in the darkness. You cannot nourish yourself solely by digging up the past. You cannot survive on vengeance alone. You need adventure, momentum, hope. You need vitality—a will to live. That's what will keep you going. That's what defines your spirit. That's what inspires you to overcome even the most impossible odds—and make the choice to live, again and again and again, choosing to reincarnate every single day. So, how will you broaden your horizons? How can you infuse your life with more joy, play, and optimism—not *in spite of* the challenges, but *because* you decide to persevere. You're not here to be miserable. It's time to reconnect with what makes you shine.

Today, I invite you to utilize fire magic. This ritual requires you to tap into your sacred inner flame. What do you desire? What ignites your passion? What makes you excited to be alive? Light a candle and gaze into the flame as you explore these prompts in your psyche. See if you can sink into a meditative state to access deeper layers of your unconscious. Allow your soul's desire to fill you with joy. Write that deep desire on a small piece of paper. Grab a firesafe bowl filled with water and set it next to your candle. Roll up the piece of paper with your intention on it, and burn it in the flame of the candle. The paper doesn't need to burn all the way through for your magic to come to fruition—even the smallest scorch yields profound impact.

If it's meant for you,
you don't have to force it;
if it's not meant for you,
forcing is futile.

Seated on a throne decorated with motifs of sea nymphs, fish, and shells, the Queen of Cups wears a blue gown and a matching cape that resembles rippling water. She contemplates an elaborate vessel she holds in her hands—it's a complex object, with a carved gold lid and handles that bow in crescent moon shapes. The Queen is situated on a pebbly shore. Calm water flows around her, near her feet. There's a powerful knowing embedded in the imagery of this card; the Queen maintains a sense of calculated privacy. Since cups represent emotion, intuition, and creativity, we know this queen is a master of connecting to her artistic, subconscious realm. But with a profile view, she's *intentionally* excluding us, creating a boundary. And that's okay. Not all feelings, emotions, and sensitivities are meant to be broadcast to the world. Not all sparks of imagination need to be disseminated. We must sit with our own feelings, thoughts, and ideas so that we can nurture and support them without the influence of external variables. Today, consider what you're privately and quietly nurturing. What are you holding close to you, and how does that thoughtful reserve make you feel? Remember that you don't need to share your brilliance, magic, or unique expressions with everyone. Keep some of your vibrant psyche just for you.

Today, it's important to be aware of how you're communicating, and what you're trying to achieve through self-expression. If you find yourself sugar-coating, tiptoeing, or omitting uncomfortable information, reground in your truth, and remind yourself that discomfort and confrontation aren't inherently bad. Conflict isn't a crime. Dissent isn't indecent. Focus on opening safe spaces for productive dialogue and remember that you have the incredible ability to elevate conversation from theory to action. It's not about avoiding disagreements; it's about taking discussion to the next level.

Don't predict the future; create it.

Be grateful for your active, intuitively guided mystical practice. Be grateful for that deep, soul connection to your truth—the gift of veracity. Be grateful for every new moon and full moon, and the tides' unique undulation. Be grateful for the planets' vibrant archetypes that punctuate your story with powerful illumination. Be grateful for the ancient wisdom. Be grateful for living mythology.

359

The King of Cups sits on a large stone throne, relatively unadorned. With an almost whale-like contour, the King's throne floats on choppy water, filled with strange sea creatures. Although the scene may appear treacherous (he is, after all, floating out at sea), the King remains calm, holding a golden cup in one hand and a scepter in the other. The King of Cups shows an intense connection to our emotional inner world. It's a reminder that even when we feel like we're in control, we're ultimately at the mercy of our psyche. Experiencing powerful and intense emotions can send us out to sea and make it difficult for us to find grounding, anchoring, or a sense of rationality. Traditionally, this card is often associated with having agency over our feelings, but it's important to maintain a thoughtful perspective when we're activated, triggered, or destabilized. Right now, consider what tools you have that help get you through these emotional, choppy waters.

360

There's something to be said for just surviving. Just opening your eyes—if only for a moment—and trusting your lungs to move oxygen through your veins. Letting your heart beat, your legs stretch, and your most basic physiological needs shoot electric signals to your brain. There's something to be said for having survived the heartbreak, the trauma, the disappointments, and the pain. That alone is heroic. That alone is worthy of praise.

361

Just as a skilled alchemist turns base metals into gold, you possess the power to transmute past wounds into invaluable wisdom. Close your eyes and visualize the person or situation you seek to forgive. Feel the emotions that arise without judgment, acknowledging their presence, experiencing their thorny complexities. Now, imagine a brilliant light enveloping your heart, radiating compassion and understanding. As you inhale, draw in this healing light; as you exhale, release resentment and hurt. With each breath, feel the weight of negativity dissipate, replaced by an aura of tranquility. Speak your intention to forgive aloud, addressing the person or situation directly. This practice won't stop the hurt—it won't wash away the very real situations that have transpired and, undoubtedly, shaped your reality. But it will give you an opportunity to breathe new life into the wounds, to aid their healing, to shift their weight. Now you can carry this new alchemical elixir with you: a testament to your capacity for transformation.

The Judgment card depicts an angel (perhaps the same figure represented in the Temperance card) who is blowing a horn, as gray figures emerge from rectangular boxes—presumably the dead rising from their graves. This card is a symbolic interpretation of Judgment Day. But rather than the judgment coming from a divine, devotional figure, this tarot card offers a personal interpretation. This card suggests that you are at the end of a very important chapter and are closing out a profound, life-changing cycle. As you aggregate all the information, wisdom, and learning you metabolized throughout this journey, it's finally time to synthesize everything you've discovered. What have you learned? How have you grown? This card is about using your emotional and intellectual processing to reflect on your experiences and to clarify whether you're truly prepared to step into the next phase of your journey. Today, consider whether you're ready to embark on a new mission or if there is still unfinished business that needs to be resolved. Consider this your personal Judgment Day.

Good things take time.

364

While it's easy to think of miracles as larger than life, grandiose happenings, remember that the Universe rarely delivers theatrics; magic manifests best through minutia. Magic is the morning sun washing over your kitchen. Magic is arriving at your destination exactly on time. Magic is belly laughter. Magic is the first snow, the first bloom, the first autumn chill. Magic is observation. Magic is hope. Magic is breath. Magic is the electricity that runs through your body, wiggling your toes and pumping your pulse with pleasure. Magic is the moments between moments—it's all the tiny details that constitute a life well lived. Magic is simply existing.

365

The last card in the tarot's Major Arcana—The World—illuminates the powerful, mystical, liminal space between an ending and a beginning. This card depicts a nude figure holding a baton in each hand, and wearing a laurel victory wreath. The four corners of the card contain the four "living creatures" of Jewish mysticism—the man, the ox, the eagle, and the lion—heavenly beings described in Ezekiel's vision. The World card symbolizes completion, an indicator of fulfillment and a job well done. It's closure. But it's also suspension. It's the completion of a cycle, the last line in a book. The feeling of driving away, leaving a place forever. It's the moment before you start anew. The World card is a reminder that for us to reenter a cyclical narrative, we must give ourselves permission to exist between storylines. This card is about being fully prepared to embrace a massive transformation. Today, consider how the World relates to your current situation. Are you in a period of transition, suspended between an ending and a beginning? Are you in a moment of metamorphosis? Are you ready to step into the portal? Of course you are. It's all magic.

ACKNOWLEDGMENTS

This work is very sacred to me, as it was conceived in tandem with my pregnancy. I wrote this book throughout my second and third trimesters, and edited it in my fourth—as I nursed my tiny Talula. Likewise, there's a special type of energy infused in these pages: a raw, unfiltered transmission generated from the creation portal. And one that couldn't have been accessed without an entire village.

First, I would like to thank my incredible colleague—Katrin Ree—for her patience, ingenuity, and fortitude. As I navigated both pregnancy and the early days of motherhood while writing this book, Katrin's brilliant dedication kept me on track and focused, even helping me translate some of my fugue-state musings and turn them into decipherable entries. Katrin, thank you for everything and more. I cannot tell you how much you mean to me, both professionally and personally. I'm so grateful the Universe brought us together.

Thank you to my extraordinary husband, Luke, for braving yet another all-consuming project. Thank you for brainstorming with me, believing in me, and always encouraging me to keep going—even when the mountain felt too steep to climb. Thank you for helping me figure out how to alchemize my creativity, coming up with practical solutions to my fantastical ideas. Thank you for keeping me fed and rested, and showing up in every possible way as a partner and—now—as a father. I love you endlessly across every lifetime.

Deep thanks to my manager, Adam Krasner, who's been cruising with me on this wild journey of a career since the very beginning. Working with you is a true gift; I love getting excited about projects together (in fact, there's something I've been wanting to chat with you about. . .) Thank you for always having my back.

Thanks to my agent, Brandi Bowles, for your continued support and enthusiasm, and for helping bring *It's All Magic* to life. Your support means so much to me.

Thank you to my editor, Anna Cooperberg, for seeing my vision! Thank you for getting it! Thank you for inviting me into the Hay House family (you know I'm such a fangirl), and transforming a concept into a finished product. Thank you for your adaptability, patience, and thoughtful guidance. This work quite literally wouldn't exist without you, and it's been a true honor visioning and crafting this book together.

I want to extend heartfelt gratitude to my community—especially members of the Constellation Club, as well as Lunar Lodge and Day Retreat attendees—who inspire me through their kindness, bravery, and dedicated practices. Thank you for sharing your stories and bringing such vital, magical energy to our sacred containers. You are all magic.

Thank you to my friends, for your love and laughter. There's nothing I adore more than being silly geese together.

Thank you to my mom, Lotti, for instilling a deep creative confidence within me that has empowered me to do this work. I'm so grateful to be your daughter; I'm the luckiest.

Thank you to my supporters on social media, who have helped me find my voice.

Thank you to all the guides, teachers, mentors, and wise ones who have expanded my consciousness.

And, finally, thank you to God, the Universe, Nature, the trees, the Sun, the Moon, and every manifestation of divinity, which is—of course—everything. What an honor to celebrate your magic.

ABOUT THE AUTHOR

Aliza Kelly is a renowned astrologer, author, columnist, and media host. She writes a column in *New York* magazine's *The Cut*, maintains a robust online community, and is the author of *The Mixology of Astrology*, *Starring You*, *This Is Your Destiny*, and *There Are No Coincidences*. Aliza has been featured in numerous publications including *The New York Times*, and is a regular guest on *The Drew Barrymore Show*. Learn more at **alizakelly.com**.

Hay House Titles of Related Interest

YOU CAN HEAL YOUR LIFE, the movie,
starring Louise Hay & Friends
(available as an online streaming video)
www.hayhouse.co.uk/louise-movie

THE SHIFT, the movie,
starring Dr Wayne W. Dyer
(available as an online streaming video)
www.hayhouse.co.uk/the-shift-movie

***

*COSMIC CARE: Astrology, Lunar Cycles and Birth Charts
for Self-Care and Empowerment,* by Valerie Tejeda

STARCODES: Navigate Your Chart with Choice-Based Astrology,
by Heather Roan Robbins

*THE ESSENTIAL TAROT JOURNAL: Record Your Readings, Expand
Your Practice and Deepen Your Connection to the Cards*

*POSITIVE MANIFESTATION JOURNAL: Inspirational
Prompts & Exercises for Creating the Life of Your Dreams*

All of the above are available at your local bookstore,
or may be ordered by contacting Hay House.

***

CONNECT WITH
HAY HOUSE
ONLINE

 hayhouse.co.uk   @hayhouse

 @hayhouseuk   @hayhouseuk

 @hayhouseuk   @hayhouseuk

Find out all about our latest books & card decks • Be the first to know about exclusive discounts • Interact with our authors in live broadcasts • Celebrate the cycle of the seasons with us • Watch free videos from your favourite authors • Connect with like-minded souls

'The gateways to wisdom and knowledge are always open.'

Louise Hay